OUTPOST OF EMPIRE

OUTPOST OF EMPIRE

THE ROYAL MARINES AND THE
JOINT OCCUPATION OF SAN JUAN ISLAND

MIKE VOURI

Published by Northwest Interpretive Association
Seattle

Distributed by University of Washington Press
Seattle and London

Published by
Northwest Interpretive Association
Seattle, WA 98104-3627, USA
www.nwpubliclands.com

Distributed by
University of Washington Press
PO Box 50096
Seattle, WA 98145-5096, USA
www.washington.edu/uwpress

Book and cover design: Mark MacKay & Ben Nechanicky

Printed in Canada by Hemlock Printers Ltd.

ISBN 0-914019-46-5

Cover photo: The Royal Marine Light Infantry (RMLI) garrison on the eve of departure from San Juan Island in November 1872 after more than twelve years on the peaceful joint occupation with the U.S. Army. The commandant, Capt. William A. Delacombe is in left foreground, while U.S. Army and Royal Navy Officers stand at left rear. Two marines remain on sentry duty at the blockhouse in the background. One of the marine's last acts was to cut down the flagpole. The United Kingdom donated a new 80-foot flagpole for the park in 1998. The blockhouse and three other structures remain as part of San Juan Island National Historical Park. Courtesy *San Juan Island National Historical Park Archive*

Back cover photo: Looking forward, toward the bow of HMS *Satellite*. Courtesy *Yale Collection of Western Americana, Beinecke Rare Book and Manuscript Library*

FOR SUSAN

CONTENTS

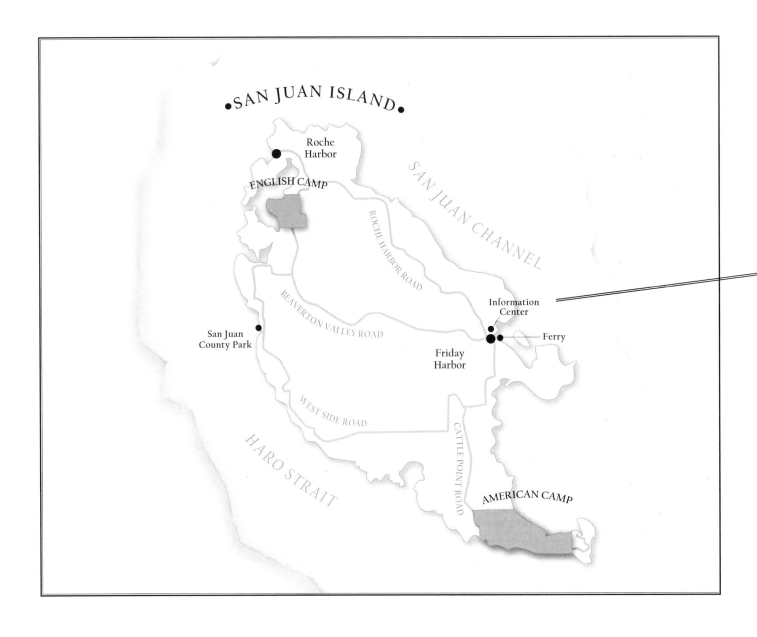

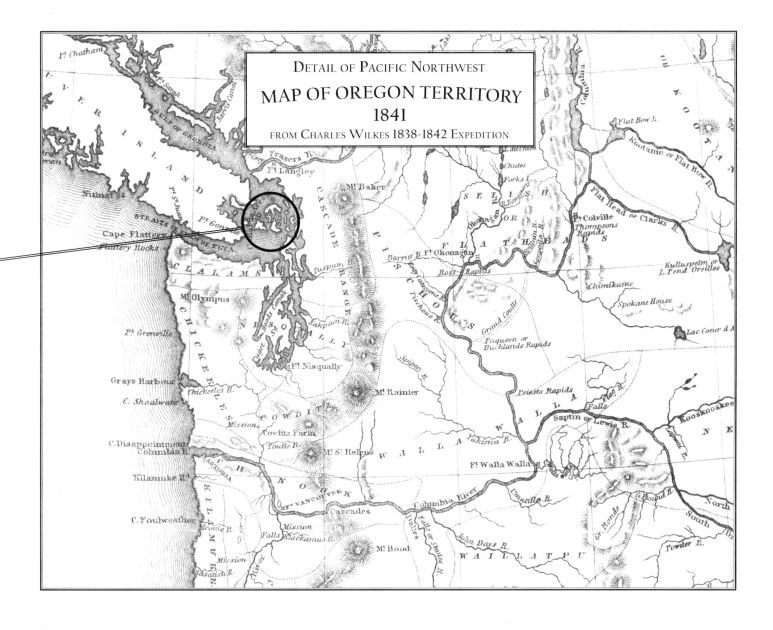

DETAIL OF PACIFIC NORTHWEST

MAP OF OREGON TERRITORY
1841
FROM CHARLES WILKES 1838-1842 EXPEDITION

Looking aft aboard Her Majesty's Ship (HMS) *Satellite*, with officers and seamen striking poses for the photographer. (inset) Captain James Prevost of HMS *Satellite* in the uniform of an Admiral. Photographed while in Germany in 1872 during the boundary arbitration.

INTRODUCTION

Her Majesty's Ship (HMS) *Satellite* steamed through Mosquito Pass and carefully made way through a series of narrow channels on the northern end of San Juan Island. Stands of evergreen and thickets of Nootka rose grew to the shoreline and rocky beaches glistened in the late afternoon sun as the 21-gun steam corvette skimmed along the flood tide. The Royal Marines on board must have been struck by the irony of this peaceful setting. For nine months prior, they had nearly been pressed into combat against U.S. Army infantry over possession of the San Juan archipelago. But cooler heads had prevailed and now the marines were, along with American troops, to jointly occupy the islands and safeguard British interests until the boundary could be determined.

The date was March 23, 1860. The *Satellite* dropped anchor in a small bay that its captain, James Prevost, had spotted the year before and recommended as a possible campsite. The boats were lowered and the marines rowed to the east shore, where stood the ruins of a native village amid mounds of clam shells, bleached white by sun and resembling drifts of snow. The marines would carve a military post from this setting, meeting challenges that must have seemed daunting at first. But the lads doffed their tunics, rolled up their sleeves and went to work, thus beginning a 12-year chapter in the history of the island and resulting in the cultural legacy of San Juan Island National Historical Park.

For nearly 60 years the Royal Navy had held sway in the Pacific basin, affecting global policies that applied throughout the 19th century. Those being: *deterrence through possession of overwhelming force, the protection of British commercial interests and the safe use of the seas.* As the military arm of the navy, the Royal Marines would remain a critical element of that mission by maintaining order aboard ship, firing muskets at the enemy from the rigging during actions at sea and bearing the brunt of combat on land. Now, the camp on San Juan Island was to reflect one more aspect of their mission—keeping the peace. The temptations of

The Hudson's Bay Company's Belle Vue Sheep Farm on San Juan Island, September 1859.

gold in British Columbia and cheap land in Washington Territory were always present, but for the most part the Royal Marine garrison remained steadfast and disciplined, and the commanding officers attuned to the policies of the Foreign Office and Admiralty pertaining to the joint occupation. Questions of national ownership had always been a flash point on the island and it was largely because of British policies of firmness and restraint that the two great nations did not go to war over an island 16.5 miles long and 6.5 miles wide.

The Royal Navy was ordered to the North Pacific and Vancouver Island in the late 1840s largely as a result of tensions between the United States and Great Britain first over possession of the Oregon Country—today's Washington, Oregon, Idaho, British Columbia and portions of Montana and Wyoming—which had been jointly occupied by the two nations since 1818. The Oregon Treaty, signed in 1846, had been drafted to resolve the problem when it divided the Oregon Country along the 49th parallel. The border would run from the Rocky Mountains through today's Blaine, Washington, down the middle of the

Old Astoria, 1854

Old Astoria Green's Store

Strait of Georgia, which divides Vancouver Island from the mainland and out the Strait of Juan de Fuca to the Pacific Ocean.

But the treaty makers in London failed to notice that the San Juan Islands bisect the Strait of Georgia into two channels—the Haro Strait running west of the islands, the Rosario Strait east. The Americans insisted on the former, the British the latter. In a hurry to sign the treaty, the nations agreed to hold the islands "in dispute" until a boundary agreeable to both nations could be divined. Unfortunately, no one thought to address the issue of jurisdiction over the islands—British or U.S., military or civil—which would be handled in a desultory and at times flammable manner.

An undercurrent of bad feelings went back to the early days of the fur trade when in 1810 John Jacob Astor's American Fur Company snatched the mouth of the Columbia River from the British Northwest Company. The Astorians had been bought out under threat of the Royal Navy during the War of 1812, but they were two decades later replaced by a stampede of American farmers, snapping up arable farmland in the Williamette Valley. By then the Hudson's Bay Company—which in 1821 had absorbed the Northwest Company and moved its headquarters 74 miles upriver to the current site of Vancouver, Washington—had

Looking forward on HMS *Satellite*.

diversified into timber, fishing and farming and was shipping its products throughout the Pacific Rim. If being driven from the banks of the Columbia and its plantations in what is now southwestern Washington were not bad enough, now, in the wake of the treaty, Americans were pushing north into the Strait of Georgia, where prairie islands beckoned.

An international incident flared on San Juan Island in January 1855 when a sheriff's "posse" from the mainland confiscated 35 breeding rams belonging to the Hudson's Bay Company-owned Belle Vue Sheep Farm. The HBC had been grazing sheep on the island since late 1853, which it had assumed granted propriety rights. American officials in Washington Territory disagreed and when they were not dispatching tax collectors, they were encouraging settlement, which moved Vancouver Island Governor James Douglas to tighten his grip. Several incidents took place, culminating in the removal of the rams, which Whatcom County Sheriff Ellis Barnes claimed covered back taxes owed by the HBC. Belle Vue Sheep Farm agent Charles Griffin called it theft, pointing out that the posse members, including the sheriff, were the only bidders at a so-called sheriff's auction on the beach below his cabin. This precipitated a flurry of diplomatic traffic, which resulted in a letter from the U.S. Secretary of State ordering U.S. territorial officials to cease and desist in harassing British subjects on the island, and prescribed a joint civil occupation.

The incident finally moved the United States Congress to appropriate funds necessary to commence a joint boundary survey with the British government. The survey work began in the spring of 1857, with Prevost and Archibald Campbell serving as the British and U.S. commissioners respectively. The two met

Brigadier General
William S. Harney

U.S. Army Soldiers freeze for a moment in front of the fledgling
encampment at Cattle Point in October 1859.

six times between June and December 1857, but could not agree on a water boundary—Prevost following specific instructions to retain San Juan Island, Campbell to claim the entire island group.[1]

A gold strike up the Fraser River swept the West Coast in 1858, drawing thousands of prospectors to the area, the majority of them from the United States. Several drifted onto San Juan Island in the winter of 1859 and by June one of them shot an HBC pig for rooting his garden. This generated a number of threats, imagined and otherwise, which resulted in U.S. Department of Oregon commander, Brigadier General William S. Harney, ordering a company of infantry, under the command of Captain George E. Pickett, to the island in July to prevent the British government from "assuming jurisdiction" over U.S. citizens. The 60-man company swelled to nearly 500 soldiers by mid-August. Douglas responded by sending several British warships, plus contingents of Royal Marines to San Juan to ensure the same. The two forces faced off on Griffin Bay for several weeks before leaders of the two nations ordered a stand down and decided upon a joint military occupation. Deciding how that occupation was to work was no easy task.[2]

JOINT OCCUPATION: Civil or Military or Both?

To cool the situation on San Juan Island and represent the U.S. proposal for a joint occupation, President James Buchanan dispatched Lieutenant General Winfield Scott, the 72 year-old commander of the U.S. Army, to Washington Territory in September 1859. Known as the "Great Pacificator" for his mediation of two similar border crises two decades before, Scott's marching instructions were clear: He was to propose a *...joint [military] occupation of the island under such guards as will secure its tranquillity without interfering with our rights.*[3]

Scott believed that the Pig War crisis had been precipitated by the frontier passions of local authorities on both sides. In his view, territorial and provincial officials tended to make arbitrary decisions based upon self-interest. That San Juan was neutral (or disputed) territory further complicated the matter, therefore:

Lieutenant General
Winfield Scott

...It strikes me as a decisive objection to this basis that if a Magistrate (Judge or Justice of the Peace) could be legally (Except by a Treaty between Sovereign Powers) established on neutral territory, such functionary could not be subjected to the orders of the United States Army, nor even to the direct control of the President of the United States, though appointed by an American territorial governor claiming jurisdiction over the disputed territory, and therefore not be considered a fit person to be entrusted with matters affecting the peace of two great nations.[4]

As a show of good faith, on November 5 Scott ordered all reinforcements from the island, save for one company, which would remain to protect settlers from both nations from Indian raids. He next established a precedent that would rule throughout the joint occupation: Territorial officials of the United States would have no jurisdiction over British subjects on San Juan Island as long as the island was in dispute. Should a British subject be caught breaking the law, particularly selling *strong liquors* to U.S. soldiers, he would be remanded to British authorities. Enclosed with the letter was a draft of a *Project of a Temporary Settlement, etc.,* that further proposed:

> *...a joint military occupation be substituted for the present one...and until that question be amicably settled shall consist of two detachments of Infantry, Riflemen, or Marines of the two nations, neither detachment of more than 100 men, with their appropriate arms only, and to be posted in separate camps or quarters for the equal protection of their respective countrymen on the island in person and property, as also to repel descents of marauding Indians.* [5]

Meanwhile, unknown to Scott, the British had already concurred with the spirit of Scott's orders. The Colonial Secretary, the Duke of Newcastle, wrote Douglas on November 16 authorizing him to act upon Scott's proposition of a joint military occupation. The following month Foreign Secretary Lord John Russell wrote the Admiralty requesting them to instruct Pacific Station Commander Rear Admiral R. Lambert Baynes to *...furnish 100 Marines, with a captain of Marines, to occupy the island on our side. The words 'appropriate arms' are understood to exclude the employment of cannon. I am to add that this arrangement is to be considered as provisional.* [6]

That same day another letter was dispatched from Russell to Lord Lyons, British ambassador to the United States, restating (and enclosing a copy of) Baynes's instructions, adding that *...Her Majesty's Government presume that in the spirit of Mr. Secretary Marcy's dispatch, there will be no exclusive jurisdiction.* [7]

From 10 to 14 days were required for word to travel from London to Washington, and six weeks more to Victoria, as neither telegraph nor Pony Express was in place in the winter of 1859-1860. Therefore,

Douglas in early November was sending missives pressing for a joint civil occupation, even to the extent of proposing an abandonment of Belle Vue Sheep Farm and leaving all of the islands between the Haro and Rosario straits unoccupied. He further stressed the economic *unfeasibility* of stationing troops upon the island because it would attract more squatters (the old HBC bugaboo). Neither government should promise to protect settlers.

Baynes concurred with Douglas at least on this point. In a letter to the Admiralty, written November 9, Baynes also was in favor of a joint civil occupation. He was wary at first of Scott's offer because, as yet, Scott had done nothing to reduce his forces on the island. Baynes wrote: *It was ridiculous to suppose that (the troops) had been placed there to protect a few American squatters from the hostile attack of northern Indians. They were evidently there as a menace to us, and until they were withdrawn, I thought it impossible to treat.*

Baynes believed that after Douglas's second dispatch, Scott felt compelled to make an overture and withdrew the reinforcements. By contrast, Baynes thought the British landing forces would indicate that British subjects needed protection, which he contended they did not:

> *Throughout this untoward affair we have been perfectly passive, exercising a degree of forbearance which their Lordships may not, perhaps, altogether approve, but called for, in my opinion, by the almost certainty of a collision at this distant point causing a rupture between the two nations; and I felt that as long as the dignity and honour of the British flag was in no way compromised, I should be best carrying out the views of Her Majesty's Government, and the interests of these colonies, by avoiding the risk of it...Acts of discourtesy on minor points were, on more than one occasion, shown by the authorities of the United States, though the military behaved with perfect propriety. This was all an irritating matter.* [8]

Indeed. Vast distances continued to sow confusion and alarm not only in the minds of Douglas and Baynes, but the home government as these letters and dispatches trickled in weeks after the joint military occupation agreement had been concluded. The perception was that Baynes (and Douglas) seemed to be dallying in establishing the joint military occupation simply because Scott had left for home and the island had quieted.

The Royal Marines garrison on San Juan Island, probably in the early 1860s.

The earthworks remain in the same unfinished state as when Lieutenant-General Scott withdrew the main body of troops, and the buildings, consisting of fourteen or fifteen shanties forming two sides of a street are almost deserted.[9]

The response to these letters from the Foreign Office is a dramatic indicator of the importance the government placed on maintaining peaceful relations with the United States. Lord Russell wrote the Admiralty, expressing the hope that Baynes *...will have landed 100 marines, under an office, upon that island without reference to the fact of General Scott having returned to Washington.* He also wrote Newcastle of the Colonial Office, observing that he could not *...but feel that Governor Douglas has incurred a serious responsibility in delaying to act upon ...instructions of the 16th of November last, and that serious consequences may ensue if the execution of those instructions is further delayed.*[10]

SITE SELECTION

———•◆•———

Baynes and Douglas, however, already were abiding by their instructions and establishing the joint military occupation, the government's original entreaties having arrived in mid January. The admiral solicited from Captain Prevost a list of appropriate locations for a camp, while Douglas queried Lieutenant Colonel Richard Moody, Royal Engineers' commander in British Columbia. Moody thought San Juan a poor choice, as it seemed to eliminate the rest of the other islands in the group from consideration in the boundary dispute. Locating the two garrisons on the same island might also ...*have the effect of dividing, even in men's minds, the Island of San Juan between military forces in occupation.* Therefore he believed that Orcas Island was the logical choice for the British garrison.

Prevost probably knew the San Juan Island shoreline better than anyone, having surveyed it since the joint boundary survey had commenced in 1857. He submitted a list of seven island locations to Baynes, each marked on a tracing of San Juan Island map. These included (1) Rocky Point on the southeast end of the island, (2) Hubb's claim, also on the southeast portion of the island where the Cape San Juan development is located today, (3) the prairie just above Eagle Cove, (4) A field just west of Belle Vue Sheep Farm's home station, about 400 yards west of the American encampment, (5) the sheep station southeast of Little Mountain, known today as San Juan Valley, (6) the current site of English Camp on Garrison Bay (apparently called Roche Harbour by the British, though not to be confused with the site of today's Roche Harbor Resort), and (7) the sheep station on the site of the future town of Friday Harbor.[11]

Prevost was cool to the Cattle Point sites because of their proximity to the U.S. encampment. He also wanted to avoid snarls with American claimants such as Paul K. Hubbs, Jr., the U.S. deputy collector of customs. Already residing on the Cape San Juan site (No. 2), Hubbs had demonstrated during the Pig War crisis that he was a personality to be avoided. Oddly enough, the Friday Harbor site seemed perfect, but

A view of Garrison Bay, ca. 1860.

Lieutenant
Richard Roche, RN.

was considered too far away from Griffin Bay to be effective. [12]

While the captain considered site No. 6 an ideal location for a camp of any size, Baynes worried about the absence of fresh water. This concern was dispelled on a subsequent trip when a *Satellite* officer, Lieutenant Richard Roche, wrote:

> *About three quarters of a mile in a SSE direction there is a large patch of water, half lake, half swamp, on the northern shore of which is a situation admirably adapted for an encampment. It slopes gently to the southwest, is well sheltered, has a good supply of water and grass, and is capable of affording maneuvering ground for any number of men that are likely to be required in that locality, there being a large extent of Prairie Land, interspersed with some very fine oak timber.* [13]

Roche's site was enhanced by two streams of water, one running from a creek draining into the south end of the bay, the other being what is called today the *Roche Harbor watershed*, emptying into Westcott Bay around Bell Point. The location also benefited from runoff from Young Hill, a 650-foot eminence rising east of the future parade ground. The marines eventually dug two cisterns on the edge of the parade to catch the runoff, which the park uses to this day to water the formal garden at the height of the dry season.

Garrison Bay indeed was a natural setting for a military encampment with a sheltered harbor and gently sloping beach front for landing of troops and supplies. A broad midden area, ideal for a parade ground, had already been cleared of large trees by the Indian inhabitants while a progression of natural terraces would facilitate additional structures. Finally, the bounty of fresh water, timber and stone provided natural resources critical to establishing and maintaining a military encampment.

Another Royal Navy subaltern, Lieutenant Richard Mayne of the survey ship HMS *Plumper*, had a decidedly different view of Garrison Bay:

'Satellite' left with Marines for San Juan. They are to live in camp on the north end of the Island, near Wescote creek. I cannot help thinking this is a great mistake after saying we would not send troops there for the last 9 months, that it was not 'English' etc. etc. to do so to cave in now, but I suppose it is ordered from home, and then sticking them at the opposite end of the Island as if they were to eat each other. I should like to see [Captain Hunt, American Camp] how he will laugh at it!! [14]

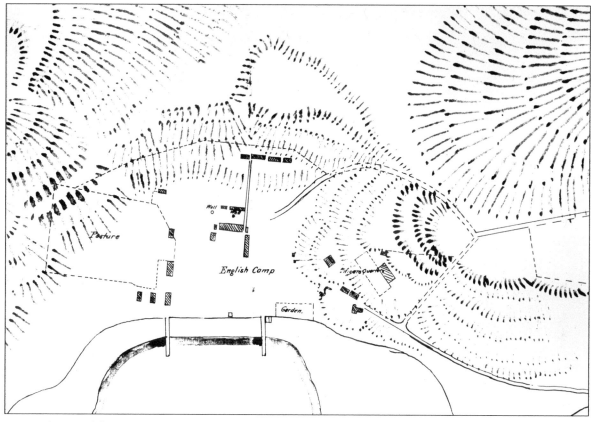

This map of the recently abandoned Royal Marine Camp, drawn in 1874 by Major Nathaniel Michler, CE, U.S. Army, reveals the topography of the camp, including the terraces constructed by the marines.

THE ROYAL MARINE CAMP, 1861

A painting by an unknown artist (facing page) dated 1861, depicts the camp as it would appear in subsequent images over the years. The barracks and blockhouse are completed, as are several other structures. The parade ground has been dramatically cut back from previous images (see page 11).[53]

A Royal Navy structure in the 1860s, most likely at Esquimalt.

A detail from the painting (opposite) showing an Indian canoe.

A map of San Juan Island showing the military reservations drawn by Captains Bazalgette and Pickett.

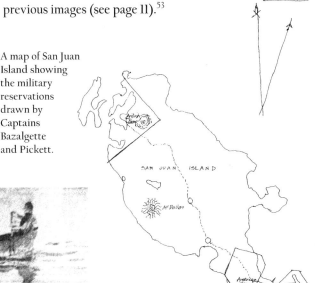

Aca. 1861 painting of the Royal Marine Camp with Young Hill in the background. Anthropologists believe the bare slope is attributable to burning by the native inhabitants of the island.

THE **ROYAL MARINES** IN THE **PACIFIC NORTHWEST**

D ouglas in 1858 had requested a stronger Royal Navy presence in the region to affirm British hegemony. More marines would help maintain the peace up the Fraser River and throughout the vast territory of New Caledonia (soon to become the province of British Columbia) after gold was struck early in the year. Since the War of 1812, the Royal Navy had regularly transited the Pacific to safeguard British commercial interests and hold Imperial Russia and the United States at bay. Starting in 1791, Russian fur traders had pushed down from the Aleutians to Sitka then leapfrogged to a post on the northern California coast. The Americans, meanwhile, had made it plain in the halls of Congress, not to mention in the boot tracks of Lewis and Clark that the new nation would stretch from sea to shining sea. But it was not until 1836 that a Pacific Station, headquartered at Valparaiso, Chile, was formally created ranging north to south from the Antarctic to Russian America (now Alaska) and west to today's International dateline. As Admiral Sir Cyprian Bridge commented, British naval power in the Pacific and elsewhere was so *ubiquitous and all-pervading that, like atmosphere, we rarely thought of it and rarely remembered its necessity of existence.*

That is, unless the navy was being wielded as cudgel to correct the balance of trade. In China, for example, British ships in 1842 and again in 1858 fought their way up the Canton River and unleashed Royal Marines on the beaches. These were the first and second Opium Wars that resulted in Hong Kong becoming a British colony until it was returned to China in 1999. [15]

The Royal Marines were founded in 1664 as a corps of sea soldiers, a sea-bourn strike force that would be raised and disbanded several times throughout the next century until the organization was permanently formed under the Royal Navy. They were officially dubbed the *Royal Marines* by King George III in 1802 following sterling service in the Napoleonic Wars, and by 1855 had been divided into light infantry or *Red Marines*, and the artillery, the *Blue Marines*. [16]

Valparaiso

Fort Victoria, British Columbia

In June 1858, Admiral R. Lambert Baynes was ordered from Valparaiso to Victoria to evaluate Douglas's request and determine how much of a naval force would be required to maintain control north of the 49th parallel. It was a good thing the orders were timely. In the period ending July 1, more than 19 steamers arrived from San Francisco with at least 10,000 miners streaming into the fields. Many of them came from a drop-off south of the 49th parallel on Bellingham Bay. In May 1858, Prevost was ordered to abandon the boundary survey and position the *Satellite* at the mouth of the Fraser. Meanwhile the ship's contingent of Royal Marines moved upriver to New Westminster, and in July as far east as the diggings at Fort Yale (today's Yale, B.C.). Here they assisted the Engineers in putting down the *Ned McGowan War*. McGowan personified the very element that Douglas feared—he was a disgruntled American whose rabble-rousing among his fellow miners had escalated into an attempt to take over the mainland government by force. Meanwhile in London, the Admiralty responded by sending the auxiliary screw frigate, HMS *Tribune* and screw corvette HMS *Pylades*, plus 164 Royal Marines. These included officers and noncommissioned officers, culled as volunteers from two battalions stationed near Canton, China.

The *Tribune* was commanded by Captain Geoffrey Phipps Hornby who had traveled overland across Asia to join the 31-gun ship, anchored in Hong Kong. The *Tribune* had successfully led an assault on a fleet of junks near Canton. Once in command, Hornby was ordered to return to Canton to embark ...*as many supernumerary Royal Marines as she can carry* and the China and East Indies Station could spare. Supernumeraries were marines not attached to a ship. Many of these supernumeraries, including Captain George Bazalgette, were bloodied in combat operations such as the taking of Canton, and the drive to isolate the capital at Peking (now Beijing). Others were seasoned combat veterans of the Crimean War and the Great Mutiny in India. Victoria Cross winner Colour Sergeant John Prettyjohn was among them. [17]

Judging from future correspondence, the men of the China brigades, officer and enlisted, were induced to *volunteer* for Vancouver Island duty by the prospect of earning colonial or extra pay. New colonies meant roads, utilities and public buildings, which in many cases were built by British soldiers, who earned wages from the Colonial Office as well as the War Office.

Spurred by this prospect, as well as an uncommunicative wife at home, Corporal Charles Whitlock of the China contingent re-enlisted for ...*the Gold diggings for Six years.*

Competition also was heavy for the commissioned posts. Royal Marines at sea were under sole authority of the ship's captain. This left marine officers in a subordinate role and contributed to their being considered *socially inferior* to naval officers. Advances in naval gunnery had made obsolete marine marksmen positioned high in ships' rigging or *fighting tops*. Shore duty, where marine commanders were sovereign, was much preferred. [18]

Brigade commander Colonel Thomas Holloway sifted through the list of applicants and endorsed five officers: Captains George Bazalgette and Thomas Magin, First Lieutenant G.L. Blake and Second Lieutenants Richard P. Henry and Edward C. Sparshott ...*in preference to the others who have offered their service.* [19]

The volunteers were shipped across the Pacific aboard the *Tribune* in November 1858 and arrived in Victoria on February 14, 1859. The accommodations on board were grim, according to Hornby:

Captain Geoffrey Phipps Hornby, RN

HMS *Tribune*

...We shall be awfully lumbered up with our 150 marines; I don't know where all the room gets to. She is 1,570 tons, her complement is only 330, and yet she only stows three months provisions...No tiers, bad storerooms, sail room, etc. I take three marine officers to sleep in my fore cabin. We shall have three or four casks between every gun on the main deck, and the Royal Marines stowed on top of them; so—as they say she is very wet at sea—they will have a jovial time of it.

Hornby had a penchant for irony. It took *Tribune* 33 days, beating against ferocious seas, to reach Nagasaki, Japan. As Francis Martin Norman, the third navy lieutenant aboard, was to write many years later:

I never made so disastrous a passage. After seventeen days struggle with adverse gales and currents we actually found ourselves nearer to our point of departure than we had been on the tenth day. The ship laboured heavily and leaked in every seam, and we were continually employed in repairing damages to sails, ropes, and rigging...Then we always had between sixty and seventy men on the sick-list, and seven died. [20]

Nagasaki as it looked in 1859.

The *Tribune's* crew and passengers spent 17 days in Nagasaki refitting from the stormy seas. The Japanese were on the cusp of profound changes in the wake of U.S. Navy Commodore Matthew Perry's visit four years earlier. Despite evidence of Europeanization throughout the city, Norman was struck by some of the more exotic aspects of Japanese culture, such as removing shoes when indoors. ...*I at once observed the wide gap existing between the great and next toe, which arises from the thong which fastens the sandal to the foot.*

While in Nagasaki harbor, Norman was sent ashore to negotiate with the Japanese governor a resting place for a *deceased* Royal Marine. Permission was given for the marine to be interred in a Russian section of a Buddhist cemetery. The funeral party was met by a delegation of monks who led the way in to the cemetery ...*intoning all the time a service of their own which they continued while ours was in progress, finally retiring with much tinkling of little bells and leaving us to finish in peace.*

Following another stormy, six-week sail across the North Pacific, the *Tribune* on approach to the Strait of Juan de Fuca, fired her boilers and steamed up the broad passage. Several hours later, the ship rounded Race Rocks and skimmed into Esquimalt Harbor, the budding Royal Navy base north of Victoria, where it was saluted by *Satellite* and *Plumper,* swinging at anchor. Almost immediately, efforts were made to relieve the ship of its burden of passengers. To this end, 33 marines gathered their kits and were dispatched throughout the station to fill vacancies among ship contingents. Others were entered as *disposable* supernu-

The HMS Ganges, the ship of the line under sail in the Royal Navy, carried the supernumerary Royal Marines on her victualing roles in 1859.

meraries on the muster books of HMS *Ganges* and checked *lent to the ship of the Senior Officer at Vancouver's Island to do duty until further orders*. Those orders took the majority of them aboard *Satellite* to the colonial mainland where they maintained a military presence amongst the miners and assisted the Royal Engineers in building the town of New Westminster. Senior naval officer Captain Michael De Courcy specified that while on land the marines would be subject to the Mutiny Act rather than the Naval Articles of War, the latter solely governing men at sea. A number of the marines, still reeling from the miseries of the Pacific crossing,

An Esquimalt navy base house similar in construction to the officers' quarters at the Royal Marine Camp.

risked the consequences of the act to bolt for the far reaches of the goldfields or cross the border for a new life in Washington Territory. [21]

Now that the marines were ashore and swinging axes, Douglas wrote the War Office asking for directions in granting the marines colonial pay—their principal reason for volunteering. Douglas believed extra wages would guard against desertion to the gold fields and blunt dissatisfaction certain to arise working adjacent to the Royal Engineers

...whose greater skills and more scientific acquirements must naturally entitle them to a higher amount of compensation. [22]

The governor's request drew a storm of missives from the Colonial, Foreign and War offices, all stating unequivocally that as no military crisis seemed to exist, there was no reason for marines to remain ashore and collect colonial pay. The War Office believed that the Army already provided adequate protection in the colony. Therefore promises of extra pay made to induce the marines to volunteer were not its responsibility. The Foreign and Colonial offices responded that it was more important to station the marines elsewhere in the empire or nearer to home. In other words, the Admiralty would be ordered to pull the supernumerary marines unless Douglas could demonstrate they were absolutely essential to the colony's security. [23]

The HMS *Satellite* and U.S. Coast Survey Steamer *Active* anchor at Boundary Bay on the 49th parallel during the Northwest Boundary Survey.

However, the ministries in London did not reckon on tensions flaring over the dead pig. Following the American landing on San Juan, Douglas ordered the marine contingent to Griffin Bay, where they stood by aboard the *Tribune*, preparatory to a possible landing. When the crisis cooled they returned to Victoria, where they built a permanent camp on the site of the current Parliament buildings. It was from this camp that they were dispatched for the joint military occupation of San Juan Island. [24]

RANK AND FILE

———•❖•———

Baynes would now have to select a commander for the sensitive San Juan post. Thomas Magin, the senior captain from the China brigades, was designated to remain supernumerary aboard HMS *Ganges*, while George Bazalgette was given the assignment ashore. The choice may have been Magin's, or perhaps he had drawn too much attention to himself by writing in protest directly to the War Office over his detachment not receiving colonial pay for their work in New Westminster. The joint occupation would require an experienced officer of circumspection, tact and restraint. [25]

Bazalgette (pronounced Bă-zăl-zhĕt) was Canadian-born and a 12-year Royal Marine veteran. He came from a military family, his father John Bazalgette being the former deputy adjutant general of Nova Scotia. Commissioned a second lieutenant at Plymouth at age 20, Bazalgette had served alternately on sea and shore duty until August 1857 when he was assigned to the 2nd Battalion in China. He saw action, was awarded the campaign medal, promoted to captain in August 1858 and shipped out for duty at Vancouver Island the following November. He would serve as commander of the San Juan contingent for nearly seven years, returning to England in August 1867. He was placed on the retirement list on Feb. 22, 1870 under Order of Council and on May 17, 1872 at his *own request*. He retired with the honorary rank of major. [26]

Of English Camp's lieutenants, the Park has records for Bazalgette's first lieutenant, Henry T.M. Cooper, and second lieutenant, Edward Charles Sparshott.

Sparshott was born in Chelsea, England, and commissioned a second lieutenant in May 1855 at age 20. He was the son of James Sparshott, a paymaster in the Royal Navy. As with Bazalgette, he was sent for supernumerary service in China in the spring of 1857, but was diverted to Calcutta in August of that year to perform garrison duty during the Mutiny. He was re-embarked for China in November 1857 and a year later volunteered for service at Vancouver Island. He served at English Camp through 1867 when he embarked for home with Bazalgette. He became seriously ill en route and died in Penge on his return to England on August 19, 1867. He was only 33 years old. [27]

A native of Old Windsor, Berkshire, England, Cooper was commissioned a second lieutenant in April 1855 at age 18. He served in various capacities at the Plymouth headquarters until embarking for China in March of 1856 aboard HMS *Calcutta*. He was involved in numerous operations during the Second Opium War, including the protection of factories and the destruction of war junks at Fatshan Creek, the assault and capture of Canton, the expedition to the north and the first assault and capture of the Taku forts at the entrance to the Peiho River, which led to Peking. Following seven years service on San Juan Island he elected to remain in the area, serving as aid de camp to the governor of British Columbia. He was placed on the retired list, at his *own request* in February 1872 and two months later was appointed collector of customs for the British settlement in Gambia, Africa. He did not survive the appointment, dying five years later. He was only 38 years old. [28]

Little is known about English Camp's enlisted ranks beyond their muster sheets, which offer cryptic accountings of place and date of birth and enlistment, occupation at enlistment and service on ship and shore. A few of the men are better known, thanks to information provided by families who remained in the area and correspondence received by families in England seeking more information about their ancestors. Most information comes from the victual and muster records kept by individual warships assigned to the Esquimalt naval base. Throughout the

The Royal Marine uniform of the 19th Century featured the distinctive scarlet tunic of British infantry - with brass buttons such as the one at left, excavated by archaeologists at English Camp in the 1970s.

25

joint occupation the supernumerary marines on San Juan Island were fed, clothed and paid on the books of vessel of the senior naval commander. As mentioned above, most of the San Juan Island marines were seasoned combat veterans drawn as volunteers from the 1st and 2nd battalions of the Royal Marines Brigade in China.

On the muster rolls marines are identified by battalion, company and division. For more than 150 years to 1884, the Royal Marines consisted of independent companies which were, for convenience, grouped into divisions. In the mid-19th century the divisions were trained and quartered at the royal dockyards in Chatham, Portsmouth, Plymouth and Woolwich. It was in these yards (or bases) that officers the ranks of captain and below were commissioned, and other ranks enlisted, into specific companies to which were attached throughout their careers. However, the relationship between a marine and his company/division was purely administrative; much as today's marines wearing identification tags. Ship detachments and shore service battalions were raised ad hoc from amongst the divisional companies. Therefore, a light infantry company might contain men from a dozen different divisional companies and this is how they were identified throughout their careers. Thus on the San Juan list William Crowcomb, was carried as a private in 31 Company of the Plymouth Division, while George Brown was a private in 90 Company of the Portsmouth Division. [29]

The supernumerary marines from China were first entered on the rolls of HMS *Tribune*. They were transferred to the HMS *Pylades*, then to HMS *Ganges*, flagship of the station, and next to HMS *Bacchante*, the senior officer's vessel. Tracking entries across these ships reveals a rough demographic of the initial San Juan Island detachment. Of the 83 enlisted men, 53 were below the age of 30, and 15 below 23. The oldest enlisted marine was John Wilson, a 41 year-old private, followed by Private George Alderman, 40, Private John Charlton, 38 and Private George Doidge, 37. Sergeant George Babbage was the oldest noncommissioned officer at 37. Of those who landed on Garrison Bay on March 21, 1860 only Private James Haynes remained when the Marines marched off on November 21, 1872. [30]

Contrary to the popular perception that British enlisted men were the *scum of the earth*, drawn or pressed from wretched pockets of the cities, about half of San Juan's initial contingent were from the West

English Camp from Garrison Bay in the late 1860s.

Country, 20 from Devon alone and 12 from Somerset. Six listed Ireland as place of birth and one Scotland. However, as an 1846 survey attests, at least ...*two-thirds of those joining the army were destitute, a fifth foolishly imagined that they would be paid for loafing and a twelfth took the queen's shilling because they were bored or wished to spite their parents.* From half to two-thirds were unskilled laborers employed in factory or industrial work, while the balance had been apprenticed to a trade such as shoemaking.

Among San Juan Island's enlisted men, Colour Sergeant John Prettyjohn earned his place in the collective memory of the corps by winning his Victoria Cross at the Battle of Inkerman during the Crimean War. Prettyjohn was born at Dean Priory in Devon on June 11, 1823. He served in the 2nd Battalion in China and was identified as a member of 3 Company, Plymouth Division. Prettyjohn left England on

March 12, 1857. En route to China he was diverted to Calcutta and the Great Mutiny. He served on San Juan Island through 1863. [31]

While Prettyjohn demonstrated upward mobility within the corps, Private Nehemiah Miles was another story. A former shoemaker, the illiterate Miles—his enlistment records were attested by his mark—was born at Fisherton, Salisbury, Wiltshire sometime in 1826. He enlisted in the Royal Marines at Poole, Dorset on June 4, 1847 and served as a private marine throughout his service, which lasted until April 27, 1869 when he was pensioned. He served in China from 1857 to 1858 and possessed five Good Conduct Badges, as well as the Baltic Medal, Crimea Medal with a clasp for Sebastopol, the Turkish Crimea Medal and the China Medal with clasp for Canton. From his enlistment record we know that Miles was 5 feet 7.5 inches with fair complexion, hazel eyes and dark brown hair. He was assigned to San Juan Island until April 16, 1868. His last several months on station and in the service were aboard HMS *Scout*. His conduct and character were judged *very good*. Miles served a total of 21 years, 328 days. [32]

Another shoemaker by occupation, though more successful as a marine, was Colour Sergeant William Joy, who kept a diary that contains a detailed description of the English Camp site on landing in March 1860. (see below) He was born in Cranton, Cranborne, Dorset in 1826 and enlisted at Poole, Dorset on September 10, 1847. Joy progressed well in the corps being promoted corporal in 1856, sergeant in 1862 and colour sergeant in 1868. He was pensioned on September 10, 1868 after 21 years service, having served in many ships and spent time in Canada and elsewhere. He received the Crimea Medal with clasps for action at Balaclava, Sebastopol and Inkermann. He also held the Turkish and China medals. [33]

Park archives also contain fragments of letters from Corporal Charles Whitlock, not only a member of the original Royal Marine garrison, but a pioneer farmer on the island. What we know of the corporal beyond the muster sheets comes from letters written to his sister and father between 1859 and 1869. Following his discharge in December of 1865, Whitlock returned to the island and established a homestead about a mile from English Camp. He was unlucky.

I am sorry to tell you that I had a very bad misfortune since you last heard from me it nearly broke me down the cattle broke my fence and destroyed all of my oats and wheat and turnips and carrots and about 10 tons of potatoes and my horse got in the bog and died and a mink came and killed all of my fowles so you see that I have had a hard rut of it the total lost was about 1 hundred pounds worth of property destroyed so that I had to sell my pigs for I had nothing for them to eat I have one sow left she will soon have young I am getting everything ready to put in another crop and try it again my heart is that way I cannot give in with one Down fall I hope it will be better this year

Whitlock next offers descriptions of houses, woodlands and other aspects of island life, but as in all his letters, the dialogue descends into rampages about his wife, the unfaithful Joanna and the fact that she had barely written him all these years. *...I was discharged on the 5th of December 1865 so Mrs. Beautiful Hore Joanna have had no money from me since nor ever will anymore.*

The former corporal evidently gave up on farming on San Juan Island as his name does not appear on the 1870 census. [34]

Two marines, Robert Smith and Richard Prowse, listed one after the other on muster sheets for more than five years, also remained in the area and their descendents live on San Juan and Vancouver islands respectively. Born in North Curry, Taunton, Somerset, Smith enlisted in December 1863 at age 18. He served seven years, 328 days and purchased his discharge for 15 pounds. He possessed two Good Conduct badges and his character was deemed *very good*. Smith first homesteaded on Spieden Island, in addition to San Juan, taking out a claim in 1875. His descendents number among two of San Juan Island's oldest families, the Nash's and Chevalier's. Prowse, a Devon native, put in 13 years, 229 days, serving at English Camp from March 10, 1868 until the camp closed. He was discharged Aug. 6, 1873. His descendents live on the Saanich peninsula of Vancouver Island, just across the Haro Strait from San Juan Island. [35]

JOINT OCCUPATION: Bazalgette and Pickett

A dmiral Baynes dispatched Bazalgette and his company to San Juan Island on the morning of March 21, 1860 and wrote a letter that same day advising the Admiralty:

> *...I embarked the detachment as per margin,* on board the 'Satellite' which ship proceeded with them on the 21st instant calling on the way at the United States' camp, for the purpose of delivering to captain Hunt, the officer commanding, a letter from me, a copy of which I enclose...* Captain Bazalgette, Lieutenant Sparshott, Lieutenant Cooper, 1 colour sergeant, 4 sergeants, 4 corporals, 1 bugler, 73 privates and Mr. T.F. Mitchell, Assistant Surgeon.* [36]

The Victoria *Gazette* reported that the *Satellite* had appeared at the entrance to Victoria's inner harbor on Wednesday the 21st and *received on board the company of Marines under Capt. Bazalgette, destined for the occupation of San Juan. The Barracks adjoining the Government Buildings are now quite deserted*, the newspaper reported. Missing on the voyage was Captain R.M. Parsons of the Royal Engineers, who had played a role in site selection and drafted a plan of the camp that would be largely complete by the end of the year. Governor Douglas believed the appearance of a sapper such as Parsons in uniform would send a message to the Americans that the site had been selected for tactical advantage, a perception he wished to dispel. [37]

Baynes's instructions to Bazalgette were precise and mirrored the guidelines Winfield Scott had roughed out the previous November. The captain was advised foremost that he was not only to protect British interests on San Juan Island, but maintain a frank and free communication with his U.S. counter-

From left, Rear Admiral R. Lambert Baynes, George Bazalgette, and George E. Pickett as a Confederate major general.

part so as not to interfere with U.S. citizens, who had *equal rights on the island*. Lawbreakers of U.S. citizenship were to be turned over to the U.S. commander for justice. The captain also was to safeguard the discipline and morale of his garrison by treating vigorously with bad influences, namely pimps and whisky sellers, and do his level best to "*...prevent any of the detachment from straggling.* [38]

Two months later, Baynes was praised for his *judicious conduct* in carrying out his orders; nevertheless James Douglas felt compelled to dispatch another friendly reminder:

> *...I have to request that you will be good enough to embody in your instructions to the officer you may place in military command such cautions as may prevent him from interfering in any way with American citizens, and advise him in any intercourse he may have with the United States' officers to adopt such bearing as may promote a good understanding and preserve harmony.*" [39]

It was an opportune communication because on the southern end of the island *Brother Jonathan* was at it again. Captain Lewis Cass Hunt, whom Winfield Scott had placed in command at Douglas's request, had been relieved and replaced with the *punctilious* Captain George Pickett. This was the officer on whom Douglas placed a portion of the blame for the Pig War crisis and who had been removed from the island by Scott in November at the governor's request. Worse, Pickett's orders stated that General Harney did not recognize the joint occupation as such. In Harney's view, the islands were part of Whatcom County, Washington Territory and *any attempt to ignore this right of the Territory will be followed by deplorable results, out of his power to prevent or control.* In other words, Pickett was to recognize the civil authority, which was totally contrary to the joint occupation terms laid down by Scott. [40]

Despite the tenor of Harney's letter, Pickett by then possessed a healthy appreciation for international diplomacy as well as the political winds at army headquarters. Following a welcome wagon visit to Camp Pickett by Bazalgette and his officers, the Virginian expressed to his counterpart *...every desire that cordial understanding, existing between you and Captain Hunt shall continue to be maintained between ourselves...* [41]

The United States government responded vigorously to Harney's actions. Secretary of State Lewis Cass assured Lyons that Harney's orders to Pickett had been revoked and that instructions were being sent west by the new Pony Express from St. Joseph, Missouri to San Francisco, which afforded *...by far the most rapid mode of communicating with the Pacific coast.* [42]

Baynes, though taken aback by Harney's orders, had decided to stand pat and on the alert, much as he had during the Pig War crisis. Orders to Bazalgette remained unchanged. He decided to ignore the general, assuring the Admiralty that

...there has existed on San Juan, since November last, so good an understanding amongst all parties, that I had intended shortly to leave Vancouver's Island to visit other parts of the Station; but under existing circumstances, I deem it more prudent to remain in the neighborhood until matters wear a more promising aspect. [43]

Soldiers of the 3rd Artillery pose with a Napoleon gun.

Matters exceeded Bayne's expectations. Harney was fired and replaced with Colonel George Wright, 9th Infantry commander, and though no formal protocols were ever written down, the island settled into the peaceful joint occupation that would last 12 years. Officials on both sides would rely on circumspection and courtesy to smooth the way, despite constant agitation by U.S. territorial officials eager to claim the islands as their own. To safeguard against that contingency, Douglas wrote:

> ...probably the easiest solution of the difficulty is to continue the joint military occupation of the island as heretofore established and...in carrying out that measure I would suggest that the Civil Magistrates, on both sides, should be wholly withdrawn, for their presence would serve to embarrass the Military Commanders; they can render them no real assistance in the discharge of their duties, as no civil jurisdiction can properly exist within the territory so long as it remains in dispute. [44]

BUILDING the CAMP

Because of greater rainfall on the northern end of the island, the English Camp site was, and is in some areas, heavily forested, principally with conifers, but also with several varieties of deciduous trees such as the Garry oak and bigleaf maple, some of the latter growing to record dimensions. The island has always been rich in shellfish, particularly in Garrison Bay, which remains a popular spot for clam digging.

In February 1860, members of the U.S. Boundary Survey had camped on the site while surveying the northern end of San Juan and Henry islands. They described the shore of a *deep inlet or bay* and believed they *were camped on the site of an Indian village.* Portions of an old lodge remained, which William J. Warren, the author of the report estimated to be *500 or 600 feet in length by about 50 or 60 feet in width and must have accommodated over a thousand Indians.* He also noted that there were immense quantities of clamshells, *usual at such localities,* and related a walk up a hill *500 to 600 feet high,* that would one day become known as Young Hill.

From this eminence we had a very extensive view. To the south and west is a beautiful valley, mostly of prairie land. At the northeastern base of the mountains is a lake about 3/4 mile in length and about 200 yards wide. Its outlet is through a swamp into the north end of the bay on which we are camped. ...The valley south of us affords excellent grazing and has been used for that purpose by the Hudson's Bay Company who has flocks of sheep on it. There are but few trees (oaks) scattered on the southern grassy slope of the mountains. [45]

The Royal Marines also were struck by the size of the midden, as well as the daunting task of clearing the land. Colour Sergeant William Joy's description of the day of landing could have been written on the boundary survey.

In 1858, the U.S. Boundary Commission erected a camp just north of the 49th parallel near today's Blaine, Washington. It was from here that teams were dispatched to survey the northern end of San Juan Island. They returned to describe the shore of a deep inlet or bay, where they camped on the site of an Indian village. A drawing of a typical Northern Straits Salish village by a survey member is depicted at lower right.

23 March 1860—Landed in a bay completely land-locked, our Camping Ground being on a shell bank - the accumulation of Years, evidently, as it averaged ten feet high, from thirty-five to forty feet through, by 120 yards long. It was the work of Indians, as they live very much on a shellfish called "Clams", and of course deposit the shells just outside their huts, hence the bank I mentioned. The brushwood grew quite down to the water's edge, in the rear the forest was growing in undisturbed tranquility, yellow Pine, White Pine, cedar, Alder and Willows in the low flat ground are the general features of the North end of the Island.

While, archaeological evidence indicates an Indian presence on the island dating to 4,500 years ago, the English Camp shell midden is of more recent vintage: from 1,400 years ago in the wooded areas and about 1,000 years ago on the parade ground; that is, a thousand years of continuous occupation. Archaeologists have identified the site as a *winter village* where the inhabitants erected wooden houses to stay out of the cold and wet. One supposition among anthropologists is that the Garrison Bay group withdrew to the mainland and/or Vancouver Island in the months immediately prior to the marine landing. Another is that they may have left in the early 1850s to escape raids by northern Indian groups, who raided in the islands to and from journeys to the Hudson's Bay Company trading post at Fort Victoria. Still another is that neighborhood had declined and the last inhabitants had moved away a generation before. A few year-round Indian communities—such as the Mitchell Bay Group, just south of Garrison Bay, and the She-Kla-Malt (Indian Tom) homestead on Lonesome Cove on the northern tip of the island—continued to exist during the joint occupation, albeit with only two or three families. At Garrison Bay, one fact was abundantly clear: No one was living there when the marines arrived in March 1860. [46]

The marines immediately went to work clearing brush, cutting trees and raking the midden to accommodate the rows of tents that would house both the officers and enlisted men over the next several months. They also dismantled the Indian house. To ensure the comfort of the garrison, Baynes had requested from Douglas a whale boat, two cooking stoves and building materials, while Bazalgette submitted a requisition for *84 tin pannikins, 36 tin plates, 3 dishes, 10 camp kettles, 18 lanterns, 1 measures set, and a small quantity of stationery.* [47]

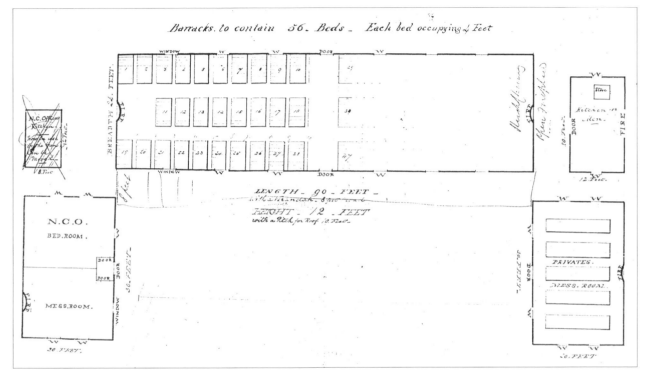

Captain Robert M. Parsons of the Royal Engineers completed these plans for the enlisted men's living arrangements in 1860. The "Private Mess Room" at lower right was expanded into a second barracks that was renovated by the National Park Service in the 1970s. Only the foundations remain of the other structures.

During a June visit, Baynes noted the primitive conditions and asked the Admiralty for an additional allowance for the men to replace clothing worn out by the timber and brush clearing. He added that they had *...not had any colonial pay since July 1859*. Baynes's request was approved, but the Admiralty specified that extra pay would be granted only for work performed *above and beyond usual duties*, which would require reports forwarded up the chain of command. These procedures were similar to the U.S. Army's, especially at frontier outposts carved from the wilderness. For the marines, for the period April-July 1859, rates were: 14 shillings a day for Captains, 9 for Subalterns, 4 for Sergeants and 3 for Privates, with a grant of land after a certain number of years.

The extra pay did not come soon enough to satisfy Charles Whitlock. In a letter home, dated March 17, 1861, he reported to his father that *I am getting very good pay, all together about seventy pounds a year.* But the extra pay had not shown up on his muster sheet: *...I have been waiting to be paid some back pay so that I would be able to send you a few pounds...I have about 30 pounds working pay to take but they have not paid it.* [48]

Baynes also ordered that a storehouse immediately be built to protect supplies and equipment during the initial phase of construction.

In late August temperatures can cool dramatically on the island, which prompted Bazalgette to write Baynes seeking proper barracks for the men *...in the event of the Detachment under my command being quartered on this island during the ensuing winter.* The captain enclosed plans for the buildings, drafted by Captain Parsons of the engineers, that he hoped would meet with the admiral's approval. They show an enlisted compound that included a 90 by 24 foot barrack with 56 beds, each allotted four feet; a noncommissioned officers' bedroom and mess; a *privates* mess room; and a *kitchen for Men* located between the barracks and privates mess room. A second sheet contains plans for a *Hospital with six beds and a Dispensary*. The admiral forwarded the request and plans to Governor Douglas on September 4. The work was in progress in October, according to Anglican Bishop George Hills, who on a visit to the camp October 10, reported *...overlooking the Bell tents & log cabins of the men, the officers quarters & mess room constituted the buildings establishment for this detachment.*

The camp plans reflected the hierarchy of military service with the officers located on the terraced hillsides and enlisted men quartered adjacent to the growing parade ground below. The camp was oriented to the bay with the barracks fronting the water about 400 feet from the beach with a mess room and cookhouse immediately adjacent. The commissary or storehouse gave onto the bay with a dock leading to its double doors to facilitate launching of the camp long boat. [49]

In addition to the barracks and commissary, the marines erected a blockhouse along the shore, ostensibly to guard against attacks from the waterside of the harbor, but in actual fact used to house prisoners. Photographic evidence indicates that they may have patterned the structure—with its upper story turned 45 degrees on the base—on the blockhouse Pickett transported from Bellingham Bay to the U.S. Army camp site at Cattle Point. Sentry boxes were positioned, also facing the bay, at either end of the beach front and an 80-foot flagpole was erected directly in front of the blockhouse.

Creating the officers' living spaces involved especially backbreaking labor excavating the natural terraces into areas spacious enough to accommodate houses and out buildings. Rocks were then gathered or extracted from the hillsides to construct stone retaining walls, which were then filled and leveled with more excavated rock and dirt, as well as tons of clamshells hauled from the midden below.

Requisition lists indicate that the marines did much of the work. Among the items were three cross cut saws, 12 spades, 50 pounds of 3-inch nails, 25 pounds of 2.5 inch nails, 25 pounds of shingles and *a small quantity of lumber for building a cooking house for the Detachment. A carpenter's chest* of tools also was ordered, as well as white lead paint, brushes and turpentine for the boat and a requisition for 20 pounds twine, 150 fathoms two-inch rope and six fishing lines. [50]

The paint for the buildings—white with yellow trim on the window frames and eaves —was manufactured from lime processed in a small kiln erected at today's Roche Harbor resort, an activity that would soon stir up the first bit of bi-national jurisdictional friction on the island. The various structures were furnished with stoves, rifle racks, clothing pegs and cupboards, all of which came from the stores of the colony. [51]

THE VEGETABLE GARDEN

Some of the best records of English Camp over its 12-year existence are visual. From the very start the camp was the subject of paintings and photographs. One taken in March 1860 shows the camp in its infancy with heavy foliage growing nearly to the shoreline as Walter Joy described. Thirteen bell tents for the enlisted men and two larger marquee tents for the officers hug the periphery of the cleared areas, while carpentry, brush cutting and gardening are in process. The vegetable garden appears in the foreground encircled by a wattle fence, with the Indian ruins in the immediate background. One marine in shirtsleeves wields a pick within the enclosure, while four others take their ease for the camera. In the background the storehouse is near completion while work proceeds on another structure, on which two men in white fatigues appear to be doing a balancing act. Meanwhile, six marines pose at attention in full dress with bayonets fixed, while others either sailors or civilians, look on with hands in pockets. A crude flagpole is positioned where the larger pole would be emplaced; the flag limp with five men in tunics at its base. [52]

The photograph above, possibly taken by Lieutenant Richard Roche, RN, captures daily life in
the Royal Marine Camp while it was under construction.

SETTLING IN TO JOINT OCCUPATION

———•◆•———

The camp soon became an attraction and tourist destination for those eager to see the islands or seeking transportation from Victoria to the mainland, and the marines seemed glad for the company. One of the earliest visitors from Victoria was Bishop Hills, a recent arrival to the colony, who called at the camp on October 10, 1860.

The bishop had been given free passage on a commercial steamer. The trip took four hours and they reached the camp at the noon hour. He described the spot as *picturesque and serene*. He was impressed by the *economy of arrangements* and most especially with the quality of the fruits and vegetables produced in the garden. The bishop would probably feel right at home on today's parade ground:

> *...deer can be had whenever wanted. Some of the post go out to shoot them, or Indians bring them." Wild fowl is abundant. There were hanging up in the larder of the kitchen geese, ducks, the common wild duck & canvas back, teal & wild muscovy. A fine wild goose can be had for a half a dollar if you buy one, later they will be made much cheaper.*[53]

After lunch Hills and Lieutenant Sparshott went horseback riding, presumably to the top of Young Hill, where the bishop was given a panorama of the island and views of Mount Baker and Mount Rainier. They then must have continued along today's Cady Mountain, where Hills claimed to see *...large flocks of sheep & settlers houses. The American Camp lay also at a distance before me some twelve miles...*

On his return the bishop found the storehouse cleared and swept, and men prepared for services, which he conducted by candlelight before returning to Victoria. [54]

Members of the American garrison were welcome as well. In fact, the two camps regularly exchanged visits on special occasions—usually the Fourth of July at American Camp, and Queen Victoria's birthday, May 24, at English Camp —a tradition begun by Pickett and Bazalgette the very first year. Newspapers of the period reported horse races on the prairie at American Camp, with Bazalgette winning the 1861 race aboard *Jerry*, while Pickett's horse bolted for the spring near South Beach. This did not preclude the two captains becoming fast friends, as they were known for visiting Victoria together.

Queen Victoria's birthday in 1866 was celebrated by the soldiers and marines, as well as 180 *excursionists*, who reached *...the beautiful and sequestered little spot* in about two hours. As Bazalgette was in Victoria attending the Governor's Ball, Lieutenant Sparshott served as host. Evidently it required more than a half an hour for the passengers to disembark and thereafter began the celebration replete with refreshments and athletic contests of ever stripe, which were open to all comers, including the excursionists, Sparshott and the post surgeon.

The wheel-barrow race blindfolded evoked intense amusement, the men rushed about in all directions and several of them disappeared, barrow and all, over the embankment...As the steamer was about to get under weigh the last game which consisted of walking a greasy pole extending 15 feet from the end of the wharf at the extremity of which was a stick three feet high with a bunch of evergreens, worth $3 to the person who could reach it came off...From the deck of the vessel the excursionists witnessed several men who attempted the perilous journey take an involuntary header into the briny deep...

At the end of the day, the group gathered *beneath the shade of a large tree* to sing *God Save the Queen* whereupon a Mr. W.K. Bull gave a speech which *...went to the hearts of the men of the garrison, who gave him three cheers.*" [55]

WHISKY, MURDER AND MAYHEM

———◆———

Most of the friction that occurred during the joint occupation usually was on the southern end of San Juan, where growing numbers of American settlers — eager to snap up land claims, sell illegal whisky and purvey prostitutes in the disputed islands — could not abide martial law. Complicating matters, the territorial government on the mainland often sided with the settlers against the local military. No such fractiousness existed between San Juan's Royal Marines and the British provincial government, especially when disputes arose with the Americans, but neither were British officials free from controversy among their own subjects.

Washington Territory's insistence on sovereignty over the islands had touched off tensions from establishment of that government in late 1853. And William S. Harney had been pleased to humor it in April 1860 by firing Hunt for shutting down San Juan Village and evicting whisky peddlers from the island. Hunt's acts were interpreted by Harney as disruption of commerce, but officials from both nations knew the general was really exacting revenge on Winfield Scott and James Douglas for overriding him during the Pig War crisis.

Pickett and Hunt had never been simpatico, especially after the latter's refusal to reimburse Pickett for buildings and stores left behind when Company D returned to Fort Bellingham the December past. But the Virginian was soon in accord with Hunt relative to the quality of his countrymen on the island. His charge from his superiors was the same as Bazalgette's: to keep intoxicating liquors and prostitutes out of his camp and guard against desertions. It was a losing fight.

San Juan Village on Griffin Bay in October 1859. The HMS *Satellite* (left) and U.S. Coast Survey
Steamer *Active* ride at anchor.

Ever since knowledge of the joint occupancy, the desperadoes of all countries have fought hither. It has become a depot for murderers, robbers, whisky sellers—in a word all refugees from justice. Openly and boldly they've come and there's no civil law over them. [56]

Through it all the commanders took advantage of the HBC-built sheep run, improving it into a military road, which , before a telegraph was installed along its track in the mid-1860s, permitted rapid transit by horse and mule power. Each commander requisitioned animals for that purpose, and when they were not doing their own riding, messengers were dispatched with missives that usually dealt with the snarls of citizenship and jurisdiction—primarily over whisky sellers, who would continue to be the bane of both commands throughout the joint occupation. Little had changed when Captain Lyman Bissell wrote in 1863, *When I assumed command of this camp in February 1862, I found the island infested with thieves and vagabonds of no particular nationality.*

Whisky traffickers and crimes attendant to their trade dominate the official correspondence of both camps. For example, in September of 1860 one John Taylor was purveying whisky to soldiers, Indians and all comers from a boat on the beach. Pickett and a squad arrived at the scene to find several Indian canoes lashed to Taylor's craft with intoxicated Indians on board. The Indians maintained Taylor was a "Boston" (American), but Taylor said he was a British subject. This was a standard ploy among San Juan miscreants. If arrested by one side, the suspect claimed opposite citizenship. Pickett interrogated Taylor and believing him a British subject, sent him packing to Bazalgette with a note that closed, *I shall be ready at any time to give my affidavit to the above facts and if necessary that of Sergeant Patrick Keanan of my company can also be obtained.*

The following year the Victoria *Colonist* reported that a Benjamin R. Spain was apprehended on the beach of the Victoria Indian reserve (presumably the Songhee settlement in the inner harbor) with a canoe-load of whisky destined for San Juan Island. Had it not been for high winds, the cargo would have been delivered, the constable claimed. The Victoria courts threw out the case for lack of evidence, but the newspaper account of the trial included a letter from to the San Juan Village barber asking *Charely and ben* to ship 40 gallons of alcohol, and if that wasn't possible then *twenty and two pounds* of brown sugar. The army responded by dispatching whisky patrols along the island's west coast (today's American Camp bluffs) *...three times a day and one at night.* The troops were to order all Indian canoes away and if they refused to leave, officers were authorized to *fire at them.*

The problem took a dreadful turn in September 1866, when the U.S. garrison commander, Captain Thomas Grey, wrote Bazalgette reporting that one of his soldiers had been *carried off* by two Indians, led by Peter of the Kanaka Bay settlement. The two also had robbed the house of a white man the day before and returned that very morning to murder him. Bazalgette reported to Grey that Peter and his followers had not been seen in the vicinity of the British garrison, nor had a marine patrol spotted him at the Indian village nearby (presumably the Mitchell Bay or Pearl Little property sites). But the marine commandant assured Grey that if he did apprehend Peter and band they would be immediately expelled. By December 1, Peter was still missing, but to insure against repeated offenses, Grey expelled the entire Kanaka Bay clan, citing not only their *insolence,* but their *...exceedingly bad habits of intemperance, thievery and the harbouring (sic) of thieves.* According to Grey, the source of these behaviors was none other than Paul K. Hubbs, Jr., under whose protection the Indians had been living and *certainly they were adept scholars of a very immoral and bad master.* [57]

The above actions underscore the open relationship between the respective commanders and their desire to assure one another of best intentions relative to the joint occupation. These intentions were especially critical in matters of jurisdiction, which had been carefully prescribed in October 1859 by Winfield Scott.

In the wake of the 1860 Taylor whisky incident, Pickett had written Bazalgette that he had (finally) read Scott's terms and sent them along with florid assurances.

> *I do not for a moment imagine that anything would have happened to disturb the perfect understanding which has existed between us both officially and personally since my arrival on the island, but I think it due to each other in the position to communicate at once any changes in orders or instructions from our superior commands.*

Communications would be critically tested that winter when a Washington Territorial issue once again (and not for the last time) spilled into the Military Road correspondence. As mentioned above, the Royal Marines in September quarried limestone and erected kilns on the site of today's Roche Harbor Resort for use in making whitewash. A sample of the product was sent to Victoria, where the Colonist reported viewing *...a splendid article of lime, white as chalk...now being made at San Juan island*. The Americans were not unaware of this vast and lucrative resource, as two months later Soloman Meyerbach (or Meyerback as it also appears), a baker residing on San Juan Island, and Paul K. Hubbs, Jr., were spotted there wielding pick and shovel. The two were undoubtedly inspired by the American-owned kilns established on the current site of Lime Kiln State Park on the west side of the island. They were apprehended by Royal Marine Lieutenant Sparshott, in company with August Hoffmeister, the Royal Marine camp sutler. Sparshott told the Americans that the limestone deposits and kilns were within the boundary of the Royal Marine reservation. Anyone caught on the site in the future would be thrown in the guardhouse by order of Captain Bazalgette. Meyerbach protested that if the British claim included Roche Harbor, it was far too large for a military reservation, being nearly 16 square miles or 64 quarter sections. Moreover, the quarry site was at least three miles away from the English Camp parade ground, and *separated by an inlet of water at least a half a mile wide*. An affidavit and petition for redress were sent to both commanders with copies filed in the Whatcom County Courthouse, and Pickett was urged by Meyerbach to *sustain* the rights of a U.S. citizen, (who is listed from Germany in the 1860 census). Bazalgette sought federal intervention from Pickett, who cautioned Americans on the island not to intrude on the British claim. He also advised his superior, Colonel Wright, to

> *...suggest to the officer commanding the British fleet the propriety of an equal reserve being laid off for each command...Should immediate action not be taken on the premises, I fear trouble will ensue.*

Marines stand at attention on the parade ground, ca. 1868.

The issue forced both nations to take steps to formally measure off their boundaries, and indeed the Roche Harbor lime deposits remained within the limits of the camp. Moreover, many of the documents in the public records pertaining to English Camp list the location of the camp proper as *Roche Harbour*. Pickett took advantage of the issue to increase the size of the American reservation so that it encompassed nearly the entire Cattle Point peninsula, save for claims around San Juan Village and Hubbs's claim at Cattle Pass. [58]

The Roche Harbor lime kiln controversy was only one of a score of incidents during the joint occupation when U.S. civilian residents protested *martial law*, and the perceived injustices perpetrated by the various U.S. commanders. Petitions were drawn and meetings held, but through it all, the army, backed by the executive branch of the government, insisted on abiding by Scott's joint occupation agreement. Such was the case in February 1863 when E.T. Hamblett, the U.S. justice of the peace at San Juan Village, organized a meeting of fellow U.S. citizens to draft resolutions insisting on civil rather than military control over the American portion of the island. The meeting was called in wake of the expulsion from the island of William Andrews, a U.S. citizen, whom Bazalgette claimed had killed an Indian in the vicinity of the Royal Marine camp, and another Indian at San Juan Village in 1860. In each case, the incumbent U.S. justice had failed to act, therefore Bazalgette pleaded with his U.S. counterpart to intervene. In the spirit of the joint occupation, a bi-national patrol, led by Bissell and Lieutenant Cooper, went to the Indian camp and learned from the head man that three of his people could identify a certain *Bill* as Andrews. The three accompanied the officers to the San Juan Lime Company at Lime Kiln, where they identified Andrews, who was in company with Augustus Hibbard, the owner. Bissell not only expelled Andrews, but posted a list of other Yankee troublemakers and gave them 24 hours to leave the island. One of them was Hibbard, who not only owned the lime works, but sold liquor on the premises and elsewhere on the island. The previous fall, Bissell wrote his superiors that Hibbard had *...tried to create a disturbance between the officers of the two camps by writing a dictatorial letter to Captain Bazalgette, because Captain Bazalgette ordered [Hibbard's] men out of his camp that went there for the purpose of selling liquor to his men.*

Hamblett's resolution and its outfall confounded U.S. military authorities at Fort Vancouver and San Francisco, spurring Department of the Pacific commander Brigadier General George Wright to state that Civil authorities, if duly appointed or elected under the laws of Washington Territory, would be permitted to exercise jurisdiction, but the joint occupation arrangements with Great Britain would be rigidly maintained. U.S. settlers wanting the protection of the army *must settle and remain within the portion of the Island within our jurisdiction.*

On receiving a copy of this judgment, Bazalgette wrote his commanding officer, Commodore James Spencer, stating he did not know what the above was about. [59]

A detail of San Juan Village from the drawing on page 45. Note the single street leading up from the Hudson's Bay Company wharf, flanked by general stores, saloons, and bordellos. The buildings, which had previously comprised a mining camp on Bellingham Bay, were barged up to the island in early August 1859, where they formed what Captain George E. Pickett termed a "... perfect bedlam day and night."

TRANSITIONS: The Camps and the American Civil War

B azalgette's friendship and collegial relationship with George Pickett ended with the outbreak of the American Civil War in April 1861. The unease among the U.S. troops at Abraham Lincoln's election and resultant secession of seven Southern states was apparent to Bazalgette during a visit to U.S. camp on February 1. On his return to the British garrison, the captain told Bishop Hills (there to conduct Sunday services) that the American officers expected a dissolution of the union and were in *a great state of excitement...but know not what will become of them.* Officers from both sections—Pickett was a Virginian, his second in command, Lieutenant James Forsyth was from Ohio—had quarreled in recent days, but had quickly made up in the face of the universal frustrations of no pay for the garrison in nearly six months and the inability to cash even Treasury bills. This was making the U.S. officers anxious because U.S. troops could legally *disband* if not paid in more than six months, Bazalgette said.

Here am I of 18 years standing, having served my Country so long, to be cast adrift! Pickett was said to have complained.[60]

Hills continued in his diary:

...The same fate awaited the U.S. Revenue Ship Massachusetts the other day at their own coal mine Bellingham Bay. The Colliery people refused to supply the coals except for cash and refused a Government Bill. The officers at the American camp San Juan are very friendly and intimate with the British Officers and they are frequently at each other's quarters.

Again, time and distance in receiving the mails, as well as confusion over whether the U.S. Army would maintain the post during the war, kept Pickett on the island through July 24. The army was still trying to decide how to apportion and consolidate its regular forces to contend with the rebellion and one solution entailed closing many of the frontier posts in the District of Columbia, including San Juan Island. Having reviewed avalanches of correspondence concerning the ever-constant issue of jurisdiction on San Juan, and citing the island's strategic location on the Strait of Juan de Fuca, Wright protested the closure to the Department of the Pacific in San Francisco. The department commander, Brigadier General Edwin Sumner, agreed and ordered the post to remain open.

Esquimalt Harbor during the mid-19th century

As usual, news of the potential closure reached England long after the issue had been settled. Rear Admiral Maitland, now in command of Pacific Station, wrote the Admiralty on June 24 wondering if the Royal Marine Camp should not be shut down as well. If so, how should he dispose of the buildings, the value of which he estimated at between 1,500 and 2,000 pounds? The response from Douglas, not to mention the home government, was swift and vigorous. The camp would remain open whether the Americans remained or not.

A MARINE'S LIFE

As prescribed by Order of Council in 1850, the daily fare usually consisted of the following: a pound of biscuit, a quarter cup of spirits, pound of fresh meat, half pound of vegetables, one and three-quarters ounces of sugar, an ounce of chocolate and a quarter ounce of tea. When fresh meats and vegetables were not available, fresh fare was substituted on every alternate day with salt pork or salt beef, flour, suet, raisins or currants. Preserved meat, potatoes or rice were also options. Once a week, the marines received a quarter pint oatmeal, half ounce of mustard, quarter ounce pepper and quarter pint vinegar (for "occasional use, as required"). Soft bread, rice, sago (breadfruit paste) and flour could be issued in place of biscuit. The ration also included a half pint of wine, a quart of strong beer and half gallon of small (or weaker) beer. Coffee, cocoa, chocolate and tea rounded out the menu.

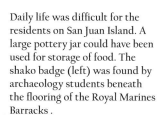

Daily life was difficult for the residents on San Juan Island. A large pottery jar could have been used for storage of food. The shako badge (left) was found by archaeology students beneath the flooring of the Royal Marines Barracks .

The Royal Marines and U. S. soldiers were also part of the local community. These items reflect some of their possible interests: an advertisement for books explaining the rules of cricket and baseball, a fancy oil lamp for an officer, a collection of shoemaker's tools and an elegant beaver hat - a high fashion style from the period.

CAMP LIFE: Food and Medicine

—◆—

While continual changes were the norm at the American post—12 commanders in 12 years—the Royal Marine camp was little changed over the next five years. Indeed, Colour Sergeant Walter Joy returned for a visit with the governor in 1865 and reported, *I found everything looking about the same as when I left it in 1863.* The men gardened, drilled and waited for mail and supplies to be dropped off by the shallow-draft gunboat that called once a month.

Occasionally, Hills would arrive to conduct Sunday services and enjoy the beauty of the island and the bounty of the Royal Marine table.

The Dinner at the Mess today proved the value of the island so far as support life is concerned.† There was excellent MUTTON fed upon the downs and shapes around.† VENISON which is always to be had for a walk in the early morning.† SALMON and a rich small member of the tribe called OULACHAN in size between a smelt and a herring caught in the bay of the settlement and DUCKS shot nearby - all produced on the Island.

The above presumably was the officers' table, as officers could afford sporting rifles and ammunition. Enlisted men's fare was carefully regulated by the Royal Navy (see pages 54-55).

The hearty meals provided fuel for marines to execute the daily drill—probably supervised in the early years by Sparshott, who wrote a manual of arms dedicated to Governor Douglas—to routinely patrol the northern portion of the island, and perform manual labor necessary to maintain the camp. This undoubtedly included hauling tons of clamshells from the midden to the hills above, where the material was

Assistant Surgeon Moss and his staff at the Royal Naval Hospital, Esquimalt ca. 1873.

combined with dirt and gravel and used to not only fill in the terraces, but reinforce trails and roadbeds leading to the main Military Road.

The sick and injured were tended by the assistant surgeon in the camp's modest hospital, depending on severity. Altogether four assistant surgeons consistently tended the company on San Juan Island throughout the 12-year joint occupation, beginning with John F. Mitchell, a supernumery assistant surgeon from the HMS *Ganges*. Mitchell already had accompanied the Royal Marine force dispatched to British Columbia to deal with the miners, so he was the logical choice for San Juan. He served two and half years before being replaced by Alexander McBride, who was followed by Ingram Hanbury and Alexander James Allen. The surgeons lived in a simple frame house on Officers Hill and practiced in the hospital structure located on the fringe of the parade ground. Little is known of the structure other than before 1868 it possessed only four beds, which had spurred Delacombe to request funds to enlarge it. By and large, the Royal Marines on San Juan Island and naval forces in general at station headquarters enjoyed good health. Anything beyond a low-grade fever or a broken arm at San Juan was usually referred to Her Majesty's Royal Navy Hospital at Esquimalt. For example, the Esquimalt surgeon, Edward Moss, recorded that Private James Manly, 27, was admitted from San Juan on October 1, 1872 with a rupture from *rolling logs*. Moss reported that Manly was fitted with a support device and discharged November 11. A drawing of the device was provided in great detail.

On his arrival to Esquimalt in 1872, Moss reported that the most common diseases in the region as *chronic rheumatism* and *paralytic diseases*. The rheumatism he attributed, in part, to the local climate:

> *There can be no doubt that the extreme variability of climatic conditions has some connection with the prevalence of Rheumatism. In this country heat, cold, dampness and dryness can almost always be found not only within days but within yards of each other.*

Paralysis was quite another matter. Some attributed it to *gold fever* or extreme excitement, as many cases were reported in the mining camps up the Fraser River. But Moss thought it might be associated with consorting with native women. Recovery ...*was the rule rather than the exception...* though often incomplete. In another entry, also made October 1, he noted that Private Benjamin Holland, 37, was afflicted with *syphilitic blotches*, and had *thin, feeble hair, quavering voice and tottering gait*. Treatment—tincture of mercury as well as other remedies—went on through December 28 and included a 10-day bout with pneumonia. The surgeon attributed the pneumonia to *the ward being unplastered* [while] *every wind passed through the chinks in the wood work of the walls making the ward very draughty and involving great waste of coal.* Though Holland's ulcers healed, Moss declared *the patient will be of little use to the service as the cure of the syphilis is hardly to be hoped for.*

Another San Juan private, George Lush, 37, was sent to Esquimalt when he complained of blurred vision. After examining the marine with an *ophthalmoscope*, Moss decided the marine's sight was *quite sufficient for ordinary purposes* and that he could *see fairly with either eye, but not with both*. Lush was ordered to take a small measure of strychnine three times a day, and to wear a shade over either eye. Slight improvement occurred and Lush was discharged to HMS *Scout* for *such duty as he could perform*.

English Camp cemetery

The climate may have been healthful, and maladies few, but nothing could help marines unable to contend with deep water. Of the seven men memorialized in the English Camp cemetery halfway up 650-foot Young Hill, four perished by drowning. Two of the seven in the fenced enclosure, Private Joseph Ellis, from Devon, and Private Thomas Kiddy, Suffolk, drowned on April 1, 1863. Both had served in the 2nd battalion in China, had crossed the Pacific in *Tribune* and were part of the original contingent in the camp. As the force was whittled down by deaths, discharges, and transfers to the fleet, men were not replaced in kind and by December 1866 the returns indicated one captain, 2 lieutenants, 3 sergeants, 2 corporals and 39 privates. [60]

THE HUGHES INCIDENT

———•◆•———

azalgette must have been growing sensitive about his declining force. On December 26, 1866, presumably after a Christmas party at American Camp, he wrote to his U.S. counterpart, Captain Thomas Grey, requesting the immediate return of a Royal Marine deserter who had been spotted in the American cantonment. Bugler George Hughes had not answered roll call at English Camp on May 22, 1861 and now he was apparently performing the same function as a U.S. soldier in Grey's company. Desertions were not all that unusual on the frontier, and men on both sides had taken *French leave* from both camps over the years lured by gold on the mainland or fed up with the isolation. Often they returned when they grew hungry enough. That Hughes would turn up in the uniform of the contending nation was so bizarre that it kicked off an international incident that went all the way to the desk of the Lord President of the Privy Council.

George Hughes is carried on the British mustering rolls as a bugler. The Devon native was part of the China battalions and an original member of the garrison who does indeed disappear from the rolls in May 1861.

On his return to the Royal Marine Camp on Boxing Day, Bazalgette agonized over what he should do in a letter to his superior, Captain Oldfield, RN, senior naval officer at Esquimalt. How should he go about seeking the return of Hughes without threatening the cordial atmosphere that had existed between the two camps? Oldfield responded by assuring Bazalgette that he was well within his rights to seek the deserter's return

Grey not only declined to return Hughes, but was taken aback by the request.

The Royal Marine Camp in December 1866.

Not recognizing that you have any legitimate grounds for requesting this soldier to be turned over to you as a Deserter, I therefore decline to comply with your request. I am not aware of your having returned to this command a deserter, therefore no one would regret the interruption of the 'good understanding which has always existed between the two camps' more than I should and I cannot but express my surprise at your anticipating in the case of Hughes any such result.

Grey acknowledged that a bugler named George Hughes was in his command, but that the man had an extensive military history, albeit one that he claimed began in 1862 with the 1st Washington Territory Infantry. In fact, he had joined the U.S. Army in January 1866 and arrived on San Juan Island in June. But despite his irritation over Bazalgette's demands, Grey continued to abide by the spirit of the joint occupation agreement by writing another letter that same day thanking the Englishman for seeking his opinion on the matter of a British whisky seller. [61] Correspondence was forwarded through channels by both commands. The response again illustrates the importance each nation placed on maintaining the peace on San Juan, especially in view of rising tensions in the post-war period over the *Alabama Claims*, and other issues. In a January 21 letter to Oldfield, Major General Henry Halleck, Pacific Division commander, promised that the case would be examined as soon as Major General Frederick Steele, commander of the District of the Columbia, returned. Meanwhile, Grey was not to enlist anyone on San Juan Island, nor was he to allow into his camp any deserter from the Royal Marines. Two months later the irritant was removed when Musician Hughes was ordered by telegraph to Fort Steilacoom. While the bugler was packing his bags, Richard Temple-Grenville, the Duke of Buckingham and Chandos and Lord President of the Privy Council had this to say:

62

> On this allegation, without rendering any proof of the identity or of the desertion Captain Bazalgette demanded not enquiry or investigation, which would have enabled him to send home a full report for consideration by Her Majesty's Government, but the surrender of an enlisted soldier of the United States Army...His Grace considers it necessary therefore to draw the serious attention of their Lords Commissioners of the Admiralty to the case in order that they may direct such instructions to be sent to Captain Bazalgette as they may deem fit to prevent reoccurrence of any similar proceedings. [62]

The above was written March 22. On April 1, Captain W. A. Delacombe, RM, and 1st Lieutenant A.A. Beadon were ordered to replace Bazalgette and Sparshott, *who have both been absent from headquarters since 1851.* Delacombe and Beadon and their *military attendants* were to travel to Vancouver via Panama by the Mail packet by April 17. [63]

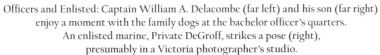

Officers and Enlisted: Captain William A. Delacombe (far left) and his son (far right)
enjoy a moment with the family dogs at the bachelor officer's quarters.
An enlisted marine, Private DeGroff, strikes a pose (right),
presumably in a Victoria photographer's studio.

THE NEW COMMANDER

William Addis Delacombe was born in 1833 in Devonshire, the son of Royal Marine General H. Ivatt Delacombe. W. A. Delacombe was commissioned a second lieutenant in July 1850 at age 17. He served with the Baltic expedition during the Crimean War in 1854, as well as in North America and the West Indies. In 1864, he won national acclaim after being dispatched aboard the HMS *Bombay* to assist in protecting British interests in Montevideo while that city was under siege by insurgents. While on station the *Bombay* was attacked and blew up at sea, with 97 officers and men perishing, 34 of them Royal Marines who died at their posts. The ship's survivors were celebrated by Parliament on their return. After the ceremony, Delacombe astounded Londoners by marching his men through the streets on their way to the barracks at Woolwich, the detachment clad in a mixture of Spanish, French and Italian uniforms given them by ships from those nations also stationed off Montevideo. Delacombe was rewarded in 1875 when, on being promoted to major, his commission was backdated to 1864 by order of the Horse Guards (Army command). Superiors also recognized his service at San Juan from 1867 to 1872 with numerous public plaudits, but a recommendation for promotion and a nomination for the order of St. Michael and St. George were not confirmed. He retired a lieutenant colonel in May 1876 and was shortly thereafter appointed chief constable of Derby from 27 applicants. He retired from the force in 1898 and died in August 1902 at his home in West Kensington. [64]

William Addis
Delacombe and his
family on the steps
of the commandant's
quarters at the
Royal Marine Camp.

THE CAMP IS IMPROVED

S hortly after Delacombe arrived, British Columbia's Lands and Public Works Department filed an inspection report on the Royal Marine Camp. While the enlisted barracks was deemed *commodious and convenient enough for all requirements* it was in dire need of repair. Brick for the chimneys needed to be reset and the floor joists were rotting away. Fireplace repairs were estimated at a cost of $50 while floors of the barracks, guardhouse (blockhouse) and storehouse could be made right for $350.

This barracks should not be confused with the current restored structure at English Camp, which has been known as *the barracks* since the national park's inception. According to the plans Bazalgette submitted to Admiral Baynes in August 1860, this structure was originally the *private's mess*. An extension was added after 1867, including built-in small arms racks, which indicates that the new commander determined to make his men more comfortable.

The officers' quarters were considered frail and not weather tight enough to withstand another winter. It was advised that they be extensively repaired or rebuilt entirely with new siding. A new house also was proposed as a residence for the commanding officer, as suggested by Captain Oldfield, the Senior Officer in command at Esquimalt.

Captain Delacombe has selected a site for such a building in the rear of and about one hundred feet above the present Officers quarter, he reported, but a well would have to be sunk for convenience. Plans were submitted for a five-room house, called a "cottage dwelling," in accordance with Delacombe's suggestions. The cost for the house, to include weatherboarding on the exterior and plaster throughout in the interior, plus two coats of paint was estimated at $2,000. Another house was to be built for Delacombe's lieutenant and his family on a lower terrace at a cost of $1,500. [65]

Meanwhile, the homeward bound George Bazalgette was in trouble with the Admiralty again, having decided to visit New York City on the way, hopefully at government expense, rather than ship directly to England from the eastern terminus of the Panama Railroad at Colon. The Admiralty would not allow it, directing the accountant general to pay the captain 108 pounds, five shillings and eleven pence, the government rate from Panama. [66]

The commandant's house was the largest and most elegant private dwelling at the camp and had a view of Haro Strait.

As Lands and Works looked after the physical plant of the camp, the Admiralty was sending a message concerning the strength of the garrison. Having noted the declining figures—47 officers and men in January 1867—the Deputy Adjutant General was directed to maintain the garrison at its originally prescribed number: 100. [67]

In addition to men, the garrison also in 1867 was issued new Enfield rifles that had been converted to breechloaders, replacing the Enfield muzzleloader in use by the marines since 1857. To maintain parity, the Americans the following year were issued the 1861 pattern Springfield rifle, also modified to be a breechloader in 1866 via what the Americans called the *Allin* conversion. [68]

THE **MCKENZIE INCIDENT**

Delacombe continued to handle the garrison and the joint occupation in a judicious manner and the camp had become a showplace on the island. Mountaineer Edmund T. Coleman stopped by in 1868 on his way to making the first Euro-American ascent of Mount Baker.

In passing along we noticed the camp of the English garrison on San Juan island, and we were struck by the singular beauty of the scenery around it. In the foreground is the level greensward with a noble tree rising from its center, and fringed with spreading maples. Up through these are the winding walks to the officers' quarters, and beyond, a lofty hill in which a summer house has been erected, where the surrounding shores are seen to advantage. Between this and the American Camp, seven miles off, lie farms in a high state of cultivation.

But all was not sweetness and light. One of those farms, elegantly dubbed the *Hermitage*, was to test the joint occupation agreement one more time. The place was located at the current intersection of Boyce and San Juan Valley roads and was being worked by Alexander McKenzie, a British subject whose naturalized American brother, Murdoch, owned adjoining acreage. But the Hermitage was, in fact, the claim of Edward Warbass, a U.S. citizen and the former U.S. Army sutler, who was away from the island at the time. Warbass had left his claim and the cabin erected upon it under the care of Angus McDonald, a former Hudson's Bay employee, who in 1867 *made an agreement* with McKenzie to crop the land until Warbass returned. McDonald died in 1868, but McKenzie stayed on, made improvements, planted and harvested crops and set up housekeeping. This happy idyll continued until April of 1870 when McKenzie was approached by August Hoffmeister, the English Camp sutler, who, acting as agent for Warbass, told

McKenzie he could have the farm for $600. McKenzie refused to acknowledge Hoffmeister as agent, and Warbass as owner, whereupon Hoffmeister returned a few days later, accompanied by an officer from the U.S. camp, who ordered McKenzie off the premises. McKenzie refused to leave, claiming British citizenship, which meant an appeal would have to be made through Delecombe.

The U.S. commander, Captain Joseph Haskell, wrote Delacombe on April 21 stating that Warbass, through Hoffmeister, had claimed American protection. He asked Delacombe to order McKenize, who was in the process of sowing another crop, to *stop plowing* and leave the property. Haskell explained that while he disapproved of *looking after special interests*, it was his duty to *look out for Creditors as well as the owner of the property.*

Angus McDonald

Delacombe responded two days later, pointing out that the McKenzie brothers (there was a third in addition to Murdoch and Alexander) were good citizens and that he knew Alexander had been in uninterrupted possession of the property for three years, *making improvements and putting up and repairing fencing and that he was in the habit of getting his brothers to help him.* Nevertheless, Delacombe agreed to order McKenzie off the property until Haskell could decide the question.

Frustrated with Delacombe, McKenzie next hired a lawyer in Victoria to take legal action against the Royal Navy for interfering with his business, which prompted Pacific Station commander Rear Admiral A. Farquhar to ask Delecombe to explain himself. The captain, while admitting McKenzie had a legitimate claim and that the brothers were *honest settlers*, was miffed that McKenzie had gone around him and hired a lawyer.

...instead of my dealing harshly with them I have gone out of my way to endeavor to prove in a measure of the truth of their statement which my letter to Captain Haskell shows, and therefore consider the course they have taken in getting some lawyer in Victoria to draw up a letter to you, after finding they could get no satisfaction from the American Authority, is most ungrateful

On June 8, Delacombe met with McKenzie, advising him that he would write Haskell for permission for McKenzie to take in his crop, but that he would still have to vacate the premises. McKenzie refused to leave, pointing out that his brother Murdoch, an American citizen, had now claimed the farm and was under U.S. protection the same as Warbass. Delacombe probably heaved a mighty sigh and rode the few miles more to the U.S. camp to verify this new information. Haskell remained adamant: He wanted McKenzie off the property. Delacombe returned to the Hermitage to find McKenzie had taken possession of the house and in a fit of pique had *turned what things it contained outside*. He also informed a marine lieutenant that he would have to be removed *by force*. The game was turning serious in Delacombe's mind. He wrote Farquhar:

I consider this man has no claim and is pitting the authority of the United States and also mine at defiance, I therefore respectfully beg you will be pleased to give me an order for his eviction from the island.

Farquhar's reply, in so many words was: *You handle it.*

Two weeks later, Delacombe dispatched an armed escort to the Hermitage. The sergeant was directed to once more order McKenzie off the property and if he did not leave, then to bring him to Garrison Bay, where Delacombe would once more try to reason with him. McKenzie came along of his own accord, Delacombe reported, and was warned that he would be evicted from the island if he persisted. When McKenzie said he did not care, Delacombe found him quarters for the night in the blockhouse. The now ex-farmer was then offered passage on the next day's boat to Victoria *of which he took advantage.*

A view of the camp just prior to Delacomb's arrival. The blockhouse
and sentry boxes are clearly defined along the waterfront.

In a letter to the Admiralty, submitted two years later, McKenzie saw it differently:

Captain Delacombe sent a Marine to me to tell me that Admiral Farquhar was at the camp to hear my case. I accompanied the man to the camp, but instead of seeing the admiral I was put into the Guard House and kept a prisoner until a boat could be procured to carry me to Victoria. Captain Delacombe told me never again to set foot on the island. My firm conviction is that Captain Delacombe expelled me from San Juan Island in order that he and Hoffmeister might appropriate the land for their own use and benefit. What I would earnestly solicit is a fair unbiased hearing.

The Admiralty was as unmoved by McKenzie as Farquhar, the issue faded away and the joint occupation proceeded unfettered. [69]

TEN YEARS AND COUNTING

—◆◦◆—

In his *State of the Station*, written in February 1870, Pacific Station commander Vice Admiral George Fowler Hastings reported the joint occupation *on the same footing as in the time of my predecessors* and that *no misunderstanding has arisen between the two camps.*

The Royal Marine camp was comprised of 84 officers and enlisted men, and while the admiral admitted that this was below the required 100 he pointed out that *...some difficulty is experienced in doing this at times without distressing the Squadron.*

By then the garrison's pay was being matched by the colony through the Foreign Office, although all monies were managed through the books of the senior officer's ship at Esquimalt. Supplies were issued through the yard's paymaster. The HMS *Boxer*, a shallow-draft gunboat capable of navigating and tying up on Garrison no matter the tide, carried provisions to the island on the first of each month. Because the waters of the Haro Strait then, as now, could be unpredictable in certain seasons, officers and their families were permitted to catch a ride to Victoria, and return on the same vessel a day or two later. [70]

Two months later, Admiral Farquhar, the new station commander, conducted an introductory inspection aboard HMS *Sparrowhawk* and declared that he was *...very much pleased (by the condition of the barracks and other buildings) and also with the state of discipline I found the men in.* Delacombe had striven to improve the daily lives of his men by erecting at *no cost to the government* a reading room and workshop. The structures were located on a terrace above the barracks, directly in line with the masonry ruin that stands adjacent to the Crook House. The admiral also ordered two new stoves to supplement the inefficient fireplaces that were located at the end of each barrack room. As chilly as the structure might have been the admiral remarked that it was decidedly superior to the enlisted quarters he found at American Camp. He also ended his report with praise for Delacombe:

HMS *Boxer*, a veteran of river actions during the Second Opium War, at the Royal Marine Camp dock.

Captain Delacombe has conducted the duties of this important command with much tact and judgement, delicate points have frequently arisen out of the joint occupation of the island, and he has always succeeded in keeping matters down, the English and American camps are on the best of terms, and a most friendly feeling at present exists between the officers. [71]

Two years later, on the eve of the settlement of the boundary dispute, the HMS *Zealous* dropped anchor in Garrison Bay. One of its officers, Lieutenant S. Eardly-Wilmot accompanied the senior officer ashore and was struck by the beauty of the site:

The English camp is picturesquely situated at the head of a beautiful little land-locked harbour, The officers' quarters—neat wooden buildings—are on the slope of a hill surrounded by gardens. The commander's house is about 200 feet higher up: a well constructed building, with offices complete and a well-filled garden, while an extensive forest close to it is an inexhaustible resource for timber and fuel.

Eardly-Wilmot pronounced the men *perfectly contented and happy*, though the men's living quarters, while comfortable could not be compared to *good barrack*. He also noted Delacombe's improvements such as the reading room, library and recreation hall, bountiful vegetable garden and fruit trees. The post seemed hardly isolated as they were regularly resupplied from Esquimalt. [72]

The cost of running camp was from $12,000 to $13,000 a year in U.S. dollars, not including pay for officers and men, as opposed to nearly double the cost for American Camp, also not including officers and men. [73]

In contrast to the mostly pleasant atmosphere on the northern end of the island, the Royal Marines' U.S. counterparts continued to wrestle with resurgent jurisdictional issues, fueled by memorials such as the petition sent by the territorial legislature to Secretary of State Seward in 1866 requesting civil jurisdiction. Territorial officials continued to believe the rule of a single military officer was arbitrary and unacceptable. American Camp's officers had been urged only to advise in squabbles, but some in sheer desperation had acted and this caused trouble.

In September of that year post commander Captain Thomas Grey and his deputy First Lieutenant William Preston Graves, both of the Second Artillery, were placed under arrest by Deputy U.S. Marshall Jared C. Brown for tearing down 150 feet of paling fence that was blocking access to the Griffin Bay dock. When the owner, the noted whisky seller I. E. Higgins, protested Grey evicted him from the island. The captain declined to go with the marshal, and the case dragged on until an appeals court threw it out in 1868. The incident prompted Major General Henry W. Halleck, now Department of the Pacific commander, in November 1867, to write the War Department and suggest placing the entire territory under martial law, or changing the boundaries of the territory to exclude the San Juan Islands. [74]

Camp San Juan Island (American Camp), ca. 1868.

JOINT OCCUPATION ENDS

F inally the two governments took matters in hand and on May 8, 1871, the Treaty of Washington was signed addressing the Alabama Claims and other outstanding issues. Among these, the British and Americans agreed to submit the San Juan question to binding arbitration under Kaiser Wilhelm (Emperor William) I of the newly constituted German Empire. The Kaiser's three-man commission voted two to one to set the boundary through the Haro Strait, thereby placing the San Juan's in U.S. territory. The emperor endorsed the judgement and a ruling was issued on October 21, 1872. [75]

Delacombe was ordered to close the camp and immediately began making preparations for departure. On Monday, November 18, HMS *Scout*, under the command of the senior naval officer, Captain R.P. Cator, arrived in Garrison Bay (which he called Roche Harbour) to withdraw the garrison and its stores, *naval and colonial*. His first business at hand was to inform Delacombe that he was to remain on the island for a few days with several *unarmed marines* and boats to certify the lands of British subjects residing there and advise his counterpart Lieutenant James A. Haughey. The loading required nearly three days. On Thursday the 21st the Royal Marines, sailors from the *Scout*, as well as Haughey and several of his officers and men stood at attention while the British colors were lowered. Department of the Pacific commander, Brigadier General Edward Canby, sent his regrets at being unable to attend and also that a U.S. warship could not be on hand to render the appropriate salute. No cannon were on hand on shore because they were forbidden as part of the joint occupation agreement. The moment was captured in a photograph, probably taken after the ceremony. The marines are arranged informally in front of the flagpole in full kit—red tunics with white cross belts, shakos, packs and rifles. Delacombe stands facing them off to the side. At left rear are Captain Cator, Lieutenant Haughey and some ladies, presumably Mrs. Delacombe and the children's nurse. Through the bare limbs of a Bigleaf maple is the blockhouse and two marines.

The Royal Marines prior to departure on November 21, 1872. Delacombe stands at left foreground in tall shako hat.

That night Cator received a telegram from the Admiralty now directing that Delacombe also be withdrawn, but offering no instructions on how to dispose of the camp. Cator was in quandary, especially after being informed that *parties of American citizens* were on their way to claim the buildings and grounds. He decided on his own to continue with the plan of leaving Delacombe behind with a few marines and wired the Admiralty accordingly the next morning. By 1872, it required hours rather than weeks to communicate with London, therefore when three days passed with no answer, and presuming the telegraph was down,

Cator decided to turn over the camp to Haughey *on behalf of the government.* Delacombe saw to the details and at 2 p.m. on the 25th , the last Royal Marines boarded the steamer HMS *Peterel* and left *Roche Harbour* for Esquimalt.

Delacombe was probably warmed by the American's last few lines:

...I now beg to express to you personally my warmest thanks for your ready co-operation with me at all times, and permit me to subscribe myself with feelings of the highest regard [76]

A small contingent, led by Haughey's second in command, First Lieutenant Fred Ebstein arrived on site on the 24th to accept the buildings from Delacombe, perform an inventory and leave a few men as a caretaker force. The inventory indicates 17 structures, in addition to the five belonging to August Hoffmeister, the English Camp sutler. The commander's, subaltern's and sergeants' quarters were pronounced in *good condition*, the barracks only *fair*, while the surgeon's and bachelor officers' quarters were deemed of *no value*, as were the guardhouse and several other buildings. Ebstein also took possession of three 200-gallon water tanks *such as are used aboard ship* and a large quantity of firewood. Hoffmeister's buildings included his store, a billiards room and the commanding officer's private stable. The U.S. contingent brought a large U.S. flag to run up the 80-foot pole, but to their surprise the pole had been chopped down. Evidently it was to be used to replace a spar lost by a British ship on a rough Pacific crossing. Old Glory instead went up the telegraph pole. [77]

The following month Haughey submitted a complete inventory of the camp to the assistant adjutant general of the Department of the Columbia, replete with dimensions, conditions and values. For example, the commander's house was 41 by 29 feet with two wings 12.5 by 29 feet each with a 12 by 20 foot kitchen attached. The house contained nine rooms in addition to the kitchen and servant room. It was constructed of frame and covered with shingles with a veranda front and rear. Haughey reported that *...the building was erected a little over four years ago and is in perfect repair.* The value? $1,000. He identified two barracks, both in good condition, each with 17 windows and two doors, valued at $600 apiece. The blockhouse was pronounced *old and worthless*. No reservation plat was available, therefore Haughey offered a detailed description, cobbled together with tape measure and compass. The entire reservation was *enclosed (except on the water side) by a stout fence.*

The last Royal Marine return for the post, filed Nov. 9, 1872, lists three officers and 88 enlisted men. The Admiralty ordered the garrison home to Plymouth, save for those who volunteered to remain on station or purchased discharges. Only six opted for the former, two for the latter, of which Robert Prowse who settled in the Gulf islands, was one. The British subjects and some U.S. citizens still residing on San Juan made a special request to BC Governor Joseph Trutch to allow Delacombe to stay on the island until the *details of relinquishment* were carried out. Delacombe remained at Esquimalt, while the petition was forwarded to London.

Meanwhile, accommodations had to be made for the transient marines. On January 1, a detachment of 20 *San Juan Marines*, including noncommissioned officers, was still quartered in the Infectious Diseases

Victoria, BC in 1858.

Ward and medical officer's kitchen of Her Majesty's Hospital, Esquimalt. The men were daily assigned to work parties at the naval yard or on the hospital wards. On one occasion it became necessary to detail two of them to assist as hospital attendants—four of them acted as sentries and were excused all other duty. Despite the help, Surgeon Moss had reservations:

> *When the detachment was quartered in the Hospital I felt it right to represent—as reported at the time—the medical impropriety of quartering men in the place where they would be most exposed to disease. I also pointed out the trouble which had followed similar proceedings during the time the Hospital was closed when the buildings were much injured and Hospital furniture destroyed. I feared—groundlessly as it turned out—that the introduction of a number of men over whose comings and goings I had no control would injure discipline of the Establishment by making the introduction of liquor easy.*

However, Moss was pleased that the marines brought their own bedsteads and used none of the hospital furniture, except the stove. And whatever inconvenience resulted from the use of the Hospital water closets was ...*counterbalanced by the readiness with which I got assistance from them in pumping water into the tanks.* When scarlet fever struck the area, the marines quartered in the Infectious Disease Ward were isolated from the rest of the naval base during an outbreak of fever. [78]

By spring, admiralty accountants estimated it would cost 1,320 pounds to ship the contingent home via Panama and authorized travel. The detachment left the hospital and joined their fellows on the 12th of May. (One marine continued on as a vegetable gardener and ward attendant.) The detachment arrived in England, sans Delacombe, on July 14, 1873.

The Secretary of the Admiralty wanted to know why Delacombe remaining behind to verify property on San Juan Island was necessary, and wired the British ambassador to the United States, Sir Edward Thorton, for an answer. Thorton wired: ...*I cannot conceive that the presence of Captain Delacombe is necessary any longer—his testimony as to their having settled upon certain lands could alone be useful to them and might be taken now.*

The Admiralty's wire to Delacombe was to the point: *Send Delacombe home to England at once.* [79]

On September 15, 1875, Department of the Pacific commander Major General John Schofield ordered the buildings at both camps sold. English Camp coincidentally had been under the supervision of a Corporal George Schofield, who had remained behind following the departure of the U.S. garrison several months before. The corporal turned over the buildings to A.E. Alden, who had been retained by the Department of the Columbia as the Quartermaster agent for both posts. His inventory, dated Jan. 3, 1875 essentially mirrors Haughey's, but without values and conditions. Auctions for the buildings at both camps were arranged for November with the English Camp buildings scheduled the 24th. The notice lists 15 structures in all at English Camp, including the commander's house. All structures, once purchased, had to be removed from the premises in 30 days. [80]

William Crook, an English immigrant, claimed the land under the Homestead Act prior to the time of the sale. The family lived alternately in several of the remaining marine structures, including the

The Wiliam Crook family claimed the Royal Marine Camp site under the Homestead Act in the mid-1870s and occupied at various times both barracks and the married subaltern's quarters. They built and moved into their own house on the grounds in 1903. At right, Mary Crook plumbs the depth of one of the cisterns the marines dug at the base of the hill on the eastern edge of the parade ground. The cisterns still exist.

subaltern's quarters and the second barracks. His son, James Crook, built a house overlooking the parade ground in 1903. They would remain on the site until the death of the youngest daughter, Rhoda Crook Anderson, in 1972.

ARCHAEOLOGY

—•◦•—

The National Park Service acquired both campsites in 1966. The first archaeological excavation at English Camp was undertaken in the summer of 1970, directed by Roderick Sprague and Robert Greengo under the auspices of the University of Washington. The purpose that first year, as stated in the contract, was to excavate in and around the four surviving structures to determine the best course in reconstruction. The site was designated: 45-SJ-24. [The designation is defined as 45 (number of state in the union), SJ (San Juan County) and 24 (the 24th designated archaeological site in the county)].

Over the next nine years a field school—primarily composed of students from the University of Idaho under Sprague's direction—excavated some 41 pits and surface sites encompassing nearly the entire living area of the camp. This was to include the barracks, commissary, blockhouse, and hospital, as well as the terraces on Officers Hill and the beach and parade ground east of the barracks. The work resulted in the recovery of 48,017 objects in all ranging from uniform buttons and shako badges, to bottles and crockery, to fragments of nails and glass. A selection of those objects is now on display at the park's American Camp visitor center. As a National Park Service unit, English Camp remains a major attraction to tourists on San Juan Island as nearly 20,000 people visit the grounds and buildings annually. Each August they can gain a taste of the joint occupation as re-enactors from the U.S. and Canada recreate on the parade ground the visits the camps exchanged a century before. They can walk through the second barracks and gaze through wavy window panes to the guardhouse, inside of which are logs hefted into place by the Royal Marines. Masonry ruins and rock walls offer hints of the hard labor that went into building the camp, while the cemetery lends a touch of pathos for those left behind.

Meanwhile, near the storehouse, a few feet under the earth, lay the original log ruins of a Salish long house, described by the first U.S. and British visitors more than 140 years before.

Such is the timelessness of English Camp.

— San Juan Island, March 14, 2004

Archaeologists excavate a pit during the University of Idaho's field school on the English Camp site in the 1970s.

The blockhouse, flagpole, and flag donated to the park by the people of the United Kingdom in 1998.

Visitors inspect the site of the commandant's quarters early in the 20th century. The monument in the foreground and a similar edifice at American Camp were erected in 1904 by the Washington State Historical Society.

NOTES

BC—British Columbia Archives

ADM—British Admiralty, Public Records Office (PRO), Kew, England

FO—British Foreign Office, PRO, Kew, England.

NA—National Archives

NAC—National Archives of Canada

SAJHA—San Juan National Historical Park Archives

WASA—Washington State Archives

Note on endnotes: Subject matter in note text is presented in order of citations.

1. British Foreign Office. San Juan Boundary: Abstract of Correspondence Relative to the Disputed Right of Territory Watered by the Oregon, or Columbia River. 1842 to 1869. December 1871. (Marked "Confidential.") This document is essentially a narrative of correspondence and documents related to the issue compiled by the British Foreign Office, pp

130-133. Vouri, *The Pig War: Standoff at Griffin Bay*, pp. 39-41; *Oxford Illustrated History of the Royal Navy*, pp. 161-163.

During the height of the Pig War crisis, boundary commissioners Prevost and Campbell exchanged a series of letters, each charging the other with duplicity and conspiracy.

The HMS *Satellite* was a 21-gun screw corvette, the largest in her class in the Royal Navy. Corvettes were flushed decked (meaning no poop or quarterdeck astern) with a single tier of guns on the upper deck. At 200 feet in length, the *Satellite* was eight feet longer than the HMS *Tribune*, a frigate and traditionally a larger class of vessel. Twenty eight-inch guns were mounted broadside, with a 10-inch chase gun on a circular emplacement at the bow. Swift and powerful, she personified the transition period between auxiliary steamers, which still relied on sail in the open sea, and warships that relied on steam power alone. Vessels of the *Satellite's* class were ideal for enforcing British policies on inland waterways such as the Strait of Georgia, and the Fraser River delta in British Columbia. Auxiliary steamers made the difference by steaming up the maze of delta waterways of the Pieho River during the assault on Canton during the Second Opium War.

British foreign policy information was taken from the *Oxford Illustrated History of the Royal Navy*, chapter "The Shield of Empire 1815-1895" written by Andrew Lambert.

James Charles Prevost (1810-1891) was the ideal choice to command the *Satellite* and serve as water boundary commissioner. He was the son of Admiral Thomas James Prevost and the son-in-law of Rear Admiral Sir Fairfax Moresby, Pacific Station commander,

1850-53. It was under Moresby's command here that Prevost, as captain of the HMS *Virago*, dealt with American miners and squatters during the brief, but intense Queen Charlotte Islands gold rush.

2. Ibid., 42-43; BC, Young to M. DeCourcy, July 23, 1859; HBC, Ft. Victoria letters out, Dallas to Griffin, July 28, 1859. The pig incident is covered in Chapter 6 of *Pig War*. In the ensuing letter traffic, Harney insisted that the British had assumed wrongful jurisdiction in the disputed territory by dispatching a ship of war to arrest Cutlar and carry him off to Victoria. While Douglas vehemently refuted the charge, there is no denying official correspondence that includes a letter from the Governor's secretary, William Young, to senior naval officer Captain Michael DeCourcy, RN, dated July 23, 1859. The missive advised DeCourcy that a commissioned stipendiary magistrate, Mr. John DeCourcy (a distant relation), had been ordered to San Juan to treat with American squatters on the island. "If possible," the governor wanted John DeCourcy conveyed to the island in a "ship of war." John DeCourcy departed July 27 aboard HMS *Satellite*, only to find Captain George E. Pickett encamped near the Hudson's Bay Company landing on Griffin Bay.

Pickett, West Point Class of 1846, is the same officer who, as a Confederate major general, led his division in the ill-fated charge that bears his name at the Battle of Gettysburg in 1863.

3. FO 14/414, Drinkard to Scott, Sept. 16, 1859. In the Buffalo-Niagara Falls incident in late 1837, Canadian reformers calling themselves "Patriots" decided on armed revolt to throw the British out of Canada. Americans south of the line provided money and weapons. Scott quickly restored calm and disbanded the U.S. military force. Two years later tensions flared on the Maine-New Brunswick border at Aroostook. The area of contention was a forest in which locals from both nations claimed harvest rights. The crisis came when respective local posses sent to apprehend "timber poachers" collided, each side capturing a man, including the Royal Warden of the Canadian province. Scott convinced both governments to return their prisoners, and revert to the status quo.

4. Ibid., Scott to Douglas, Nov. 2, 1859.

5. Ibid., Scott to Douglas, Nov. 16, 1859.

6. Ibid., Newcastle to Douglas, Nov. 16, 1859; Hammond to Admiralty, Dec. 22, 1859.

7. Ibid., Russell to Lyons, Dec. 22, 1859.

8 Ibid., Douglas to Newcastle, Nov. 9, 1860; Baynes to Hammond; to Admiralty, Nov. 9, 1859.

9. Ibid., Admiralty to Hammond, March 20, 1860; Baynes to Admiralty Jan. 26, 1860.

10. Ibid., Hammond to Admiralty, March 22, 1860; Hammond to Elliot, April 21, 1860.

11. Ibid., Baynes to Douglas, March 2, 1860, Moody to Douglas March 13, 1860.

12. FO 14/414, Baynes to Douglas, March 2, 1860; Thompson, pp 199-200). During the Pig War crisis, Hubbs, as deputy collector of customs, had insisted that British officials pay customs duties on personal baggage brought ashore. As they were to do time and again during the joint occupation, U.S. military officials intervened on the British behalf.

13. NAC., FO 5/815, Baynes to Douglas, March 17 & 19, as quoted in Thompson, p. 200; and Wood, pp. 114-115.

Roche was probably more familiar with the San Juan Islands than any other British officer. He was a midshipman aboard HMS *Herald* in 1846-47 during surveys of the Strait of Juan de Fuca by Capt. Henry Kellett. He also served with Kellett in 1852 during the search for Admiral Sir John Franklin's lost arctic expedition.

14. BC Archives, Richard Charles Mayne, Journal kept in HMS *Plumper*, Feb. 17, 1857—Dec. 31, 1860, MS handwritten in bound volume, 1 inch thick, as quoted in Thompson, p. 98.

15. Gough, pp. 2 & 29; Blumberg. Valparaiso harbor in Chile was a safe haven for ships that transited the Straits of Magellan or sailed around the Horn (Tierra del Fuego). It was also a popular port of call for the British and American whaling fleets. As such, it was the scene of one of Great Britain's few naval victories over U.S. frigates during the War of 1812. On March 28, 1814, HMS *Phoebe* and HMS *Cherub* attacked the USS *Essex* in alleged neutral waters of the harbor and pounded her into submission with their long guns. The *Essex* had been wreaking havoc with the British whaling fleet in the Pacific when *Phoebe* and *Cherub* rounded the horn in company with HMS *Raccoon* and the Northwest Company trading ship *Isaac Todd*. The British flotilla had been on its way to the Columbia River to take Astoria from its namesake U.S. fur trading company. Only the *Raccoon* eventually crossed the notorious river bar, but by then the post already had been sold to the Northwest Company by the resident Astorians. The *Raccoon's* captain took the post as a prize anyway and renamed it Fort George. Thus it would remain until the Hudson's Bay Company merged with the Northwest Company in 1821. The HBC closed the post in 1824, relocated it 74 miles upriver and renamed the operation Fort Vancouver.

The British and Chinese clashed after the British government eliminated the East India Company's monopoly of the China trade, and aggressive newcomers introduced opium from India in lieu of paying silver for Chinese goods. The First Opium War started in 1839 and ended in 1842 when the Chinese paid an indemnity of L20 million and ceded Hong Kong to the British. The Second Opium War broke out in 1856 when the Chinese seized the British merchant vessel *Arrow*. The British responded by bombarding and then capturing Canton and using steam warships and marines to neutralize Chinese forts along the Canton and Peiho rivers, which effectively isolated Peking (today's Beijing). Another British-dictated peace forced the Chinese to accept Christian missionaries deep in her interior, foreign delegations in her capital, foreign customs agents and legalization of the importation of opium—stinging blows that were not rectified until the next century.

16. Royal Marine Museum, *The History of Britain's Sea Soldiers*, pp. 2-9.

17. Gough, 134-149; Blumberg. The Great Indian Mutiny of 1857-58 was ignited in May 1857 following years of poor administration and bad treatment of Indian sepoys (soldiers) employed by the East India Company. The eruption of violence was blamed on the Company's introduction of rifled muskets that required cartridges greased with cow or pig fat, anathema to Hindus and Muslims alike. The rapid advancement in naval ordinance included high velocity, in some cases rifled, guns that could destroy an enemy ship from a mile or more off and preclude boarding. This resulted in Royal Marines aboard being little more than a police force with the officers as constables. In fact, some retired marine officers, such as William Delacombe, became chief constable when he returned to England.

18. Thompson, p. 94-97, Whitlock correspondence, Blumberg, Vol. 3.

19. ADM 30/309, Baynes to Admiralty; Blumberg; SAJHA, Whitlock correspondence.

20. Edgerton p. 52; Norman, pp.222-229; Lambert, *Oxford Illustrated History of the Royal Navy*, pp. 209-210. The *Tribune* was designed by William Symonds, a noted English marine architect, to be a 28-gun frigate (6th Rate), but in 1850 the plans were modified to make her a 31-gun auxiliary screw frigate, one of only 12 in the Royal Navy in 1859. Symonds's ships were usually swift and broad of beam, but also were "wet," as Hornby wrote, meaning they rolled copiously, which not only admitted tons of seawater, but made the guns almost useless in high seas. Steam propulsion had been practically applied to merchant shipping as a primary source of power since the 1840s. However, military steamers continued to rely primarily on sail on the open seas to ensure independence from coaling stations. Propeller-driven "combination" vessels such as the *Tribune* were powered by low compression, side-lever engines that were challenged by heavy seas and headwinds. Therefore the term "auxiliary screw steamer." As with the *Satellite*, the engines were mainly used to negotiate inland waters and transit harbors. For example, on her arrival at the mouth of the Strait of Juan de Fuca, the *Tribune* raised her collapsible smokestack, dropped her propeller into the water and steamed up the strait and into Victoria harbor.

21. ADM 30/309, DeCourcy to Young, April 12, 1859; Norman, pp233-246. Hornby would prove his mettle as a sailor and captain on the voyage. On one "wild night" on the leg to Japan, he scrambled up the mizzen to help the crew furl the mizzen topsail: "...it was the first and only time I ever saw a captain go 'above the dead-eye,' " said Francis M. Norman, a navy lieutenant. More than 600 men were stuffed into a vessel that was only 192 feet from stem to stern, which created no end of disciplinary problems. The crew being "slack" from too many months in port, Hornby literally cracked the whip to bring order. This and the attraction of gold resulted in more than 40 desertions of sailors and marines in the weeks following their arrival in Victoria.

22. FO 14/414, Douglas to War Office, April 29, 1859.

23. Ibid., War Office to Douglas June 16, 1859; Hammond to Merivale, June 16, 1859; War Office to Colonial Office, Aug. 13, 1859.

24. Thompson, p. 97; ADM30/309, Baynes to Admiralty; SAJHA, Whitlock correspondence; NA Canada RG8, Series IIIB, vol 37 .

25. BC Archives, K/RS/Sa5.

26. ADM 196/59, Bazalgette file.

27. ADM 196/60, Sparshott file. The Great Indian Mutiny, 1857-1858, swept British garrisons in India

28. ADM 196, Cooper file; Oxford Royal Navy, pp. 181-182. Fatshan Creek was located in the maze of islands lying below Canton. It was here on July 1, 1857, that British Commodore Henry Keppel, with 20 gunboats and a contingent of Royal Marines attacked and destroyed 77 of 80 war junks that were protecting the route to the city. It was hard, close-in fighting with the marines boarding the junks in turn or slogging through the mud ashore. In the end, the British toll was 84 killed and wounded. The Taku forts flanked the mouth of the Peiho River, which led to Peking, and had been reinforced by the Chinese. They were abandoned and immediately reoccupied and strengthened by the Chinese in the fall and win-

ter of 1858. After negotiations collapsed, the British lost 93 killed and 111 wounded during an assault in June 1859, whereupon, in concert with France, overwhelming force was applied. The forts fell, Peking was taken and the stage was set for the collapse of an ineffectual and irrelevant Chinese monarchy 60 years later.

29. SAJHA, Robertson to Pettus, Jan. 9, 1962; Cordingly, *Billy Ruffian*, pp. 40-52. Two other dockyards were located at Deptford and Sheerness. Dock yards throughout the 18th and 19th centuries were bustling commercial centers. Chatham, located on the Medway River encompassed more than 70 acres of docks, ship-building ways, shops, storehouses, barracks and parade grounds—all encircled by stout walls and armed guards, which proved insufficient to stop pilferage.

30. ADM 38/5647, HMS *Bacchante*, 1 Jan.—31 March 1861; ADM 38/5649, HMS *Bacchante*, 1Oct—31 Dec. 1861; ADM 38/7211, HMS *Sutlej*, 1Oct.—31 Dec. 1865; ADM 38/7428, HMS *Zealous*, 1 Oct.—31 Dec 1871.

31. James, pp. 292-293; Blumberg; ADM 38/5467.

At Inkerman on Nov. 5, 1854, then-Corporal Prettyjohn's platoon attacked a cave occupied by snipers. They took the cave but depleted their ammunition, whereupon Prettyjohn ordered the men to use rocks to beat back an expected counterattack. The Russians attempted to creep up the hillside in single file, but were repelled by Prettyjohn who seized the first Russian in line and threw him down the slope. The others were greeted by a hail of stones and retreated. Prettyjohn's medal and bayonet are on display at the Royal Marine Museum in Plymouth.

Also during the Crimean War, 25 officers and 988 enlisted men landed to fortify the heights overlooking the River Tchernaya (Marine Heights). The Marines were to protect the rear and flank. Their tents were old and dilapidated and the men suffered from the cold and damp and bad food. They fought in plain site of the famous Charge of the Light Brigade on Oct. 20, 1854.

32. ADM 157/483, Miles. Good conduct badges meant more money—sergeants receiving 15 pounds for the medal, corporals 10 and privates 5.

33. ADM 157/475, Joy.

34. SAJHA, Whitlock correspondence. Among the descriptions of island life: "Dear sister I must describe the mink to you the mink is a small animal like a stoat or a pole cat ferret but a little larger they get in the fowele houses at night and they will kill every one if they are not disturbed they only suck the blood and then leave them I had sixty killed in one night I lay wait for him and shot him...Dear sister you wished to know what of houses we have here but I can't hardly describe them to you for there are as many sorts of them in the towns the houses are built of brick and stone the same as at home but in the country places they are chiefly built with logs joined together at the corners (of wood) and no up stairs to them a man that want a house here just look for a place where he can till some land and then he will take his axe and go to the woods and cut his timber and build his house in about a week..."

35. SAJHA, Smith discharge papers; Prowse clippings.

36. FO 14/414, Baynes to Admiralty, March 21, 1860.

37. BC Archives, *Victoria Gazette*, March 22, 1860, Parsons to Moody, March 23, 1860; and Young to Parsons, March 20, 1860. It is believed that Parsons later visited the campsite in mufti to complete the drawings that bear his signature.

38. FO 14/414, Baynes to Admiralty, March 28, 1860, Inc. #3 Instructions to Bazalgette.

39. Ibid., Hammond to Admiralty, May 17, 1860; Douglas to Baynes March 17, 1860.

40. Ibid., Pleasonton to Pickett, April 10, 1860. The term "Brother Jonathan" dates to the Revolutionary War, when General George Washington sought advice from Jonathan Trumbull, governor of Connecticut. It was used by the British throughout the 19th century to refer to Americans individually and collectively.

Captain Lewis Cass Hunt, West Point, 1847, was born into a three-generation U.S. military family. His grandfather was Colonel Thomas Hunt, the U.S.'s longest serving Revolutionary War soldier, who fought as a Minuteman at Lexington and Concord and was in command of the First Infantry regiment when he died in 1808. His father, Lieutenant Samuel Hunt, died when Lewis was two years-old. He and his ten-year-old brother, Henry J. Hunt, were sent to live with their Uncle John Hunt in Maumee. Henry J. Hunt, an 1839 West Point graduate, is famed as commander of artillery for the Army of the Potomac during the Civil War. Ironically, he laid down the barrage that decimated Pickett's division at Gettysburg. Further illustrating Old Army connections, John Hunt had been a business partner of Robert Forsyth, whose son James Forsyth was Pickett's second in command on San Juan Island.

41. Ibid., Pickett to Bazalgette, April 30, 1860.

42. Ibid., Lyons to Russell, June 24, 1860. Hunt was born at Fort Detroit where his father was stationed at the time; therefore it is likely he was named for the territorial governor, Lewis Cass, a close family friend and War of 1812 hero, who remained in that office until 1831. Cass went on to become a United States senator, 1848 Democratic presidential candidate, Secretary of War, Secretary of State and minister to France.

43. Ibid., Baynes to Admiralty, May 5, 1860.

44. Ibid., Baynes to Admiralty, May 5, 1860.

45. Sprague, p. 3; NA RG76, E198, Warren journal; and Stein, pp. 53-72.

46. SAJHA, Joy diary; Stein, pp. 60-65; Stein, pp. 53-72; Boxberger, pp. 28-37. Joy's reference to "clams" seems to indicate that he was not familiar with that name for the species. Garrison Bay today has several varieties of clams, including Manila and native littlenecks, butter, horse, soft shell, geoduck and cockle. Perhaps at home he only knew them as cockles. The bay also has Pacific oysters and mussels.

These suppositions are based on the author's discussions with the ethnologist, Dr. Wayne Suttles, and UW archaeologist, Dr. Julie Stein. Among the Northern Straits Coast Salish groups who claim San Juan Island as an ancestral home are the Lummi from the U.S. mainland, and the Cowitchan, Saanich and Songhee from Vancouver Island. Ethnologists have identified 23 dialects of the Coast Salish language, nine east of the Cascades and the balance on the West Coast. The 1870 census records that of the 448 residents on the island, 163 (36 percent) were Indian, but of these only two were Indian men, listed as shepherds. Of the remaining 161, 49 were women married to non-Indian men. During the summer fishing season as many as 1,000 Indians from throughout the region would come to island to fish off the western shores. The Hudson's Bay Company would pay one blanket ($4) for every 60 fish. For an excellent account of prehistoric settlement on the island, see Stein's *Exploring Coast Salish History: The Archaeology of San Juan Island*.

47. BC Archives, K/RS/Sa5.

48. SAJHA, Charles Whitlock correspondence 1859-1869 excerpts, RM Museum, Eastney Barracks, Southsea, Hampshire, England "San Juan Island" Archive. 17/17/14; ADM 12/686.

49. BC Archives K/RS/Sa5/NAC RG8, Series IIIB, Bazalgette to Baynes, Aug. 29, 1860; Baynes to Douglas, Sept. 4, 1860; Baynes to Admiralty June 23, 1860; Admiralty to Baynes, Aug. 14, 1860; *the British Colonist,* Sept. 13 & 22, 1860, as quoted in Thompson, p. 203; Bagstraw, Hills Diaries, pp. 242-244; NA RG567, Pickett to Hardie, Aug. 28, 1860. Bell tents, similar to the U.S. Army's Sibley tents, accommodated 11 enlisted men. Officers were usually quartered in marquees, or "wall tents."

50. BC Archives, K/RS/Sa5, SAJU Correspondence. Because of exposure to saltwater, the blockhouse lower story has been rebuilt several times over the years, the last in 1995. The upper section is sealed to preserve the structure and protect visitors from the lead-based paint used by the marines.

51. BC Archives, K/RS/Sa5, SAJU Correspondence, Bazalgette requisition, Nov. 2, 1860; NA RG393, Dept. of Oregon Letters Received, as quoted in Thompson p. 203.

52. Beinecke collection, MSS S-1817. As British light infantry, the Royal Marines wore a single-breasted scarlet tunic (or jacket) with brass buttons down the front and navy-blue trousers with a 1-inch red welt (stripe) along the outer seam. Accessories included blacked boots, shako (a tall hat with badge), and white waist and cross belts on which were affixed cap and cartridge boxes and bayonet. They carried the 1853 pattern (three-band) Enfield rifled musket, which was about four feet long and weighed $9\,^1\!/_2$ pounds.

53. SAJHA, H-34-19-1-10(38); BC Archives, PDP 2616.

54. Bagstraw, pp. 242-244.

55. *Port Townsend Register,* June 27, 1860 and July 17, 1861; *the British Colonist,* May 26, 1866, as quoted in Thompson, p 104-106; Bazalgette and his "Jerry" took two out of three races the following July 4, a day in which "...the betting was lively, but for small amounts." As the San Juan Lime Company, on the north end of the island, was entertaining its employees, "several familiar faces were missing."

56. NA RG567, Pickett to Hardie, June 1, 1860; NA RG 383, Hunt to Pleasonton, March 30, 1860. Hunt ostensibly was undone by a petition submitted by San Juan Village whisky sellers distressed by his eviction of several of their number from the island, as well as by the four square-mile military reservation he established from the Camp Pickett flagpole. But the root of his conflict with Harney was his appointment by Scott. He compounded the friction by penning letters uncomplimentary to Harney's character and having them published, anonymously, in regional newspapers.

57. NA RG567 MF, Pickett to Bazalgette, Sept. 9, 1860; Pickett to Babbitt, Sept. 1, 1860; *the British Colonist,* May24, 1861; Grey to Bazalgette, Sept. 6, 1866; Bazalgette to Grey, Sept. 10, 1866; Grey to Finkbonner, Dec. 22, 1866; Bazalgette preferred horses. Pickett requisitioned the more sturdy and dependable army mules for the task.

The Peter incident is another example of an entire community being blamed for the acts of one miscreant. It is unknown if this was the Kanaka Bay settlement of employees of Belle Vue Sheep Farm, founded by the Hudson's Bay Company in 1853. The farm ceased being an HBC operation by 1866. It is a known fact that Hawaiians and some Indian people inter-married. This may be why Grey reported Peter's acts and the expulsion to Sub-agent Finkbonner on the Lummi Reservation, who had guardianship of all Indians in the area.

58. NA RG567, Pickett to Mackall, Dec. 3, 1860; Bazalgette to Pickett; Petition of S. Meyerbach to Commanders of U.S. and British forces; *the British Colonist*, Sept. 25 and 28, 1860. Meyerbach, in his deposition taken in Whatcom, contended that Hoffmeister at first meeting had claimed the quarry for himself under U.S. preemption laws. It was only later that Bazalgette maintained that the land and mineral rights belonged to the Crown.

Lime was mined at several locations on the island during the joint occupation. The "San Juan Lime Company" was founded on the current site of Lime Kiln State Park (on the west side of the island) in 1860 by the firm of Cutlar, Newsome and Gillette. Gillette sold his share to Augustus Hibbard in 1861, after which Hibbard bought out Cutlar and Newsome in 1864. Hibbard sold the company in 1865, then bought it back in 1868. A receipt for $10 for 20 barrels of lime appears in the camp letter book, signed by Lyman Cutlar (now an employee) and dated June 18, 1869. When Hibbard was shot by a disgruntled employee in 1870, the current American Camp commander, Captain J.T. Haskell, posted guards at the kiln until ordered to leave the kiln and their ownership to the civil courts.

Possibly the above enterprise spurred Meyerbach and Hubbs to do a little claim jumping.

59 NAC RG8, Series IIIB Vol. 36; Official Records; BC Archives, Bazalgette to Spencer, May 12, 1863; Hills Diaries, Feb. 1-3, 1861. Bissell's rejoinder to the resolutions is ripe with thumbnail character studies of San Juan leading U.S. citizens, also included the following: Higgins, the postmaster "lives by dealing his poisonous liquor to my men, thereby destroying them for usefulness."

60. ADM 38/3532; Walter Joy Diary; ADM38/7120; ADM 201/38; Hills Diary, Feb 1-3, 1861; ADM101/201; Lentz, pp52-62. The National Park Service has maintained the cemetery and its four original headstones since the late 1960s. However, in 1903 and as recently as the 1930s letters appeared in the Globe and Laurel, the Royal Marines periodical, reporting the deteriorating condition of the plots and seeking donations for the cemetery's upkeep. James Crook, owner of the property when the park service took over in 1966 and now deceased, claimed he received a stipend from the British Government to maintain the cemetery.

"Oulachan" (euchalon), also known as candlefish, is a variety of smelt found along the coast from Oregon to Alaska. The fish is so rich in oil at spawning time that it can be burned as a candle. The HBC shipped tons of it throughout the Pacific Rim.

On his departure Hills described, "A lovely morning, clear sky and bright sun. The beautiful scenery, the placid lake like bay and well ordered quarters of the settlement were the pleasing view from my window."

61. NA RG567, Bazalgette to Grey, Jan. 4, 1867; Grey to Bazalgette, Jan. 5, 1867.

62. NAC, RG8, Series IIIB, Buckingham to Admiralty, March 22, 1867; Halleck to Oldfield, Jan. 21, 1867, Pacific Station Records 1859-1872; NA RG567, Grey

to Bazalgette, Dec. 29, 1866; NA RG617, Reel 1112/Post Returns for Camp Steele, March 1867. Throughout the American Civil War, British shipyards and brokers had been providing commerce raiders to the Confederate Navy, which decimated the U.S. merchant and whaling fleets. The most famous and successful of these was the CSS *Alabama*. The United States wanted restitution and Britain had thus far refused to pay. The issue became known as the "Alabama Claims" and was not settled until the Treaty of Washington of 1871.

The transcontinental telegraph to Washington Territory was completed in 1864, with first message sent by Governor William Pickering to President Abraham Lincoln on September 7, 1864.

63. ADM 201/38, Deputy Adjutant to Admiralty, April 1, 1867; Admiralty to Deputy Adjutant, April 8, 1867. Delacombe was permitted to bring his wife, nurse and four children. The fares for the latter five were to be deducted from Delacombe's wages.

64 *Globe and Laurel*, 1898 edition.

65. BC Archives, K/RS/Sa5, Lands and Works to Admiralty, June 18, 1867.

66. ADM 201/38, Admiralty to Deputy Adjutant General, July 24, 1867.

67. ADM 201/38, Admiralty to Deputy Adjutant, Sept. 13, 1867.

68. ADM 201/8, Admiralty to Deputy Adjutant, Nov. 5, 1867.

69. NAC, April 21, 1870 Haskell to Delacombe; April 28, 1870, Delacombe to Haskell; May 11, 1870, McKenzie to Farquhar; May 15, 1870, Delacombe to Farquhar; May 19, 1870, Farquhar to McKenzie, copy Dela-combe; June 20, 1870, Delacombe to Farquhar; June 24, 1870, Delacombe to Farquhar; November 7, 1870, Testimonial to Admiral Farquhar. McKenzie had friends among U.S. citizens, as well as British subjects, on the island, as a petition was circulated attesting to his good citizenship. About a third of these also signed a petition that lauded the character of Delacombe and requested that he remain to protect their interests immediately following the boundary settlement. See Addenda.

70. MG12—ADM 1/6151, NAC, report of Admiral Hastings, Feb. 22, 1870. The *Boxer* appears at the English Camp wharf in a photograph taken sometime after 1867. HMS *Boxer* was a veteran of the assault on Canton during the Second Opium War.

71.. ADM 201/38, Farquhar to Admiralty, May 6, 1870. In recent months NPS crews discovered the foundations for these buildings as well as a much eroded saw pit, located adjacent to the carpenter's shop. The ruins of these fireplaces remain today on the parade ground, perfectly aligned and about 90 feet apart.

72. Eardly-Wilmot, pp. 42-44

73. Hanzard's Parliamentary Debates, 199, 1238; NA RG49, Halleck to AAG, Jan. 13, 1868, as cited in Bancroft, p. 638 n.

74. 40th Congress, pp. 266-268.

75. Miller, Northwest Water Boundary, pp. 31-67.

76. ADM 201/38 159796 San Juan papers. Documents connected with evacuation of San Juan Island by and return to England of the Detachment recently stationed at that island.

77. NA RG94, Canby to Haughey, Nov. 27, 1872; NA RG393, Ebstein to Haughey, Nov. 27, 1872;

the British Colonist, Nov. 26, 1872; NA RG393, Haughey to AAG, Dec. 15, 1872. The British claimed the pole was chopped down to replace a spar lost by a vessel crossing the North Pacific. Rumor had it that it had been chopped up and distributed as souvenirs.

78. ADM 101/281, Surgeon Moss.

79. NAC 5-1475, Admiralty to Thorton, July 14, 1873; Thorton to Admiralty July16,1873 ; Admiralty to Commander, Pacific Station, July 21, 1872; SAJHA. The petition, dated November 17, 1872, and addressed to Gov. Joseph Trutch, British Columbia, was signed by the following individuals: Robert Firth, Robert Douglas, Alexander Ross, William Bell, Patrick Gorman, Daniel Ross, Isaac Sandwith, William Douglas, William Kiddy, George Fox, Joseph Friday, Robert McLachlan, John Bull, Thomas Quinland, Stafford Merrifield, J. Archambould, Charles Barnie, Samuel Haiton, Isa Passillion, Louis Kerriere, Peter Frichetti, Charles McMillian, A. McNaughton, John Stephens, Benjamin Neeland, Daniel McLaughlan, Edward Hitchins and Benjamin Hughes. Friday and Bull were Hawaiian shepherds, who had once been employed as shepherds for Belle Vue Sheep Farm. Friday Harbor, the only incorporated town in San Juan County, is named for Joe Friday.

Many of the same people above were on a list of those declaring their intention to become United States citizens. The declaration was submitted to the U.S. District Court in Port Townsend on Jan. 13, 1873, less than two months after the departure of the Royal Marines.

80. NA RG94, Schofield to AAG, Sept. 15, 1875; RG393 Box 1, Alden statement, Jan. 3, 1875.

81. Sprague, pp. 3-15.

BIBLIOGRAPHY

Studies

Boswell, Sharon A. and Hudson, Lorelea. Heritage Resources Investigations at the Limekiln Preserve. San Juan County Land Bank, Friday Harbor, Washington, 2001.

Boxberger, Daniel L. San Juan Island Cultural Affiliation Study. MMS, San Juan Island National Historical Park, Friday Harbor, Washington, 1993.

Lentz, Florence K. Historic Furnishings Report: British Camp Hospital San Juan Island National Historical Park. Seattle: Cultural Resource Division, Pacific Northwest Region, National Park Service, Department of the Interior, 1990.

Sprague, Roderick, ed., San Juan Archaeology. Moscow: University of Idaho, 1983.

Thompson, Erwin N. Historic Resource Study: San Juan Island NHP. MMS, San Juan Island National Historical Park, Friday Harbor, Washington, 1972.

Newspapers

British Columbia Archives

Port Townsend Register, July 17, 1861

Victoria Gazette, Dec. 7, 1859

———, March 21, 1860

———, March 22 , 1860

The British Colonist, Sept. 13, 1860

———, Sept. 22, 1860

———, Sept. 25, 1860

———, Sept. 28, 1860

———, May 24, 1861

———, July 8, 1863

———, May 26, 1866

———, Nov. 26, 1872

Documents

Government

National Archives, Washington, DC, College Park, MD

NA RG49 Abandoned Military Reservation File

NA RG76, E198 Journal of William J. Warren, Secretary, Northwest Boundary Commission, of an expedition in company with Dr. C.B.R. Kennerly, surgeon and naturalist, to the Haro Archipelago.

NA RG94, Records of the Office of the Adjutant General

NA RG567 MF Reel 406, Consolidated Correspondence, Camp San Juan Island

NA RG617, Reel 1112, Returns from U.S. Military Posts,

1800-1916, Roll 1112, Post Returns for Camp Steele, March 1867, San Juan Island, Washington Territory

Official Record of the War of Rebellion, San Juan Island Correspondence, 1861-1865, Series L. Pacific Campaign

National Archives of Canada, Ottawa, Ontario

RG8, Series II B, Micro. Reel C-12616, Admiralty, Pacific Station Records 1859-1872

MG12, 5-1475—ADM 1/6151, Records pertaining to San Juan Island

British Columbia Archives

K/RS/Sa5 San Juan Island papers

Washington State Archives, NW Region

3rd District Court, 1854-1873

Public Records Office, Kew, United Kingdom

FO 14/414 Correspondence Pertaining to San Juan Island

ADM 38/3532 Mustering records from Her Majesty's Ships

ADM 38/3532

ADM 38/5647

ADM 38/5649

ADM 38/7120

ADM 38/7211

ADM 38/7428

ADM 157/271 Personnel files

ADM 157/475

ADM 157/ 483

ADM 201/38 Settlements: papers from nine overseas posts 1809-1878

ADM 201/380

ADM 201/38 159796, San Juan papers

ADM 12 Digests, 1855—1862, Vancouver's/San Juan Island

ADM 12/670

ADM 12/686

ADM 12/702

ADM 101/281

Journal of Her Majesty's Hospital Esquimalt

Pacific Station

Edward L. Moss Surgeon

Between 1 January and 31 December, 1873

Private Archives

Archives of the Anglican Provincial Synod of British Columbia and Yukon

Diaries of Bishop George Hills, 1858-1864

Government Publications

U.S. Congress. Senate. Executive Document No. 29. 40th Cong., 2nd Sess. Report of the Secretary of State. Washington, D.C.: 1867-1868.

British Foreign Office. San Juan Boundary: Abstract of Correspondence Relative to the Disputed Right of Territory Watered by the Oregon, or Columbia River. 1842 to 1869. December 1871. (Marked "Confidential.") This document is essentially a narrative of correspondence and documents related to the issue compiled by the British Foreign Office.

National Park Service, Pacific West region. Cultural Landscape Inventory, 2004, English Camp, San Juan Island National Historical Park (draft).

Other Documents

Joy, Walter, Journals. Portsmouth City Museum, England, United Kingdom. San Juan Island NHP Archive.

Robertson, A. MacGregor, Captain, Royal Marines, Historian,. Royal Marines Barracks, Eastney, Southsea, Hants, England, letter to Terry Pettus, Seattle, Wa, 9 January 1962. San Juan Island NHP Archive.

Whitlock, Charles. Correspondence 1859-1869, excerpts, RM Museum, Eastney Barracks, Southsea, Hampshire, England.

San Juan Island NHP Archive.

Views of the Pacific Northwest. Yale Collection of Western Americana, Bienecke Rare Book and Manuscript Library, WA MSS S-1817, Box 6, Folder 32.

The Globe and Laurel, 1898 edition (Journal of the Royal Marines).

Books

Bagstraw, Roberta L., editor. *No Better Land: The 1860 Diaries of the Anglican Colonial Bishop George Hills.* Victoria, B.C.: Sono Nis Press, 1996.

Bancroft, Hubert Howe, *The Works of Hubert Howe Bancroft,* reprint, New York, McGraw-Hill Book Co., n. d.32 History of British Columbia, 1792-1887.

Blumberg, General Sir H.E., KOB. *History of the Royal Marines, 1837-1914, Royal Marines Historical Society Archives Series, Vol. 3.*

Coffman, Edward M. *The Old Army: A Portrait of the American Army in Peacetime 1784-1898.* New York: Oxford University Press, 1986.

Eardly-Wilmot S., Lieutanent, ed., *Our Journal of the Pacfic by the Officers of H.M.S. Zealous.* London: Longmans, Green and Co. 1873.

Edgerton, Mrs. Fred, *Admiral of the Fleet,* Sir Geoffrey Phipps Hornby, Edinburgh, 1896.

Gough, Barry, *The Royal Navy and the Northwest Coast of North America, 1810-1814.* Vancouver, B.C.: University of British Columbia, 1971.

Holmes, Richard. *Redcoat: The British Soldier in the Age of Horse and Musket.* New York: W.W. Norton & Company, 2001.

James, Lawrence. *Warrior Race: A History of the British at War.* London: Abacus, 2001.

Hill, J.R., ed. *Oxford Illustrated History of the Royal Navy.* Oxford: Oxford University Press, 1995.

Norman, Francis Martin. *"Martello Tower" in China and the Pacific in H.M.S. Tribune 1856-60.* London: George Allen, 156, Charing Cross Road, 1902.

Stein, Julie K., *Exploring Coast Salish Prehistory: The Archaeology of San Juan Island.* Seattle: University of Washington Press, 2000.

Vouri, Michael, *The Pig War: Standoff on Griffin Bay.* Friday Harbor, WA: Griffin Bay Bookstore, 1999.

Pamphlets

The Royal Marine Museum, *The Story of Britain's Sea Soldiers.* Royal Marines Estney, Southsea, Hampshire, 1989.

RMLI at Royal Marine Camp

San Juan Island—1860-1861

⬥ denotes not part of 1st and 2nd battalions dispatched from China

★ denotes carried on San Juan Victualing List, HMS *Bacchante*, 1 January-31 March 1861

✳ denotes carried on San Juan Victualling List, HMS *Bacchante*, 1 October-31 December 1861

✴ denotes still on San Juan Victualling List, HMS *Sutlej*, 1 October-31 December 1865

✺ denotes still on San Juan Victualling List, HMS *Zealous* 1 October-31 December 1871

PO: Portsmouth Division   **PL:** Plymouth Division   **CH:** Chatham Division

WO: Woolwich Division   **Co.:** company enlisted   **b.:** badge

Also listed place and year of birth

H.M.S. *Ganges* 1 Oct.—31 Dec. 1860

✴ ★	J.F. Mitchell, Assistant Surgeon	27 Dec 60 Bacchante, Sv. at San Juan Island
★	John Bremmer, Assist Paymaster 2nd Class	24 Dec 60 Bacchante, Sv. at San Juan Island
✴ ✺ ★	Geo. Bazalgette, Captain	27 Dec 60 Bacchante, Sv. at San Juan Island
✴ ✺ ★	E.C. Sparshott, 2nd Lt.	
✴ ★	H.T.M. Cooper, 1stLt.	
✴ ✺ ★	Geo. Babbage, Sergeant, 1st. (PL), 31 Co., Devon, 1823, 1b. (Colour Sergeant in 1865)	
✴ ★	Joseph Bate, Sergeant, 1st. (PL), 71 Co., Devon, 1833,	
✴ ★	Henry Johnstone, Sergeant, 2nd. (PO), 18 Co., Middlesex	

	John Tearle, Sergeant, 2nd. (WO), 12 Co., Each, 1828, 2b.	
★ ★	Joseph Major, Corporal, 2nd. (PL), 55 Co., Devon, 1825, 20	24 Dec 60 (promoted Sergeant by Oct 61)
★ ★	John Wilson, Private, 2nd. (PO), 2 Co., Devon, 1819, 3b.	
★ ✸ ★	George Westall, Private, 1st. (CH), 61 Co.,Berkshire, 1827, 1b.	24 Dec 60
	William Hayes, Private, 1st. (CH), 81 Co., Wiltshire, 1836	8 May 60 San Juan Island
★ ★	Abraham Abbott, Private, 1st.(WO),100 Co., Worthing, 1836, 1b	27 Dec 60 Bacchante, Sv. at San Juan Island
★ ★	George Connor, Private, 1st (WO),92 Co., Dublin, 1828, 2b.	
★ ★	John Tomlinson, Private, 1st.(WO), 60 Co.,Leicester, 1836, 1b.	2 Dec 60
★ ★	George Hobbs, Private, 1st. (PL), 11 Co., Somerset, 1837	27 Dec 60
★ ★	Joseph Goddard, Private, 1st. (PL),103 Co., Lancaster, 1836	
★ ★	Thomas Cree, Private, 1st. (PL), 103 Co., Antrim, 1837	
★	John Brown, Private, 1st. (PL), Devon, 23 Co., 1837	
★	Thomas Clarke, Private, 1st. (PL), 35 Co.,Armagh, 1835, 1b.	13 June 60 San Juan Island
★ ★	George Clements, Private, 1st. (PL), 39 Co., Devon, 1838	27 Dec 60 Bacchante, Sv. at San Juan Island
	John Bryant, Private, 1st. (PL), 47 Co.,Somerset, 1834, 1b.	13 June 60 San Juan Island
	John Adams, Private, 1st. (PL), 47 Co., Dumbarton, 1837	
★ ★	Alfred Harper, Private, 1st. (PL), 99 Co.,Somerset, 1830, 1b.	27 Dec 60 Bacchante, Sv. at San Juan Island
★ ★	Thomas Conway, Private, 1st. (PL), 3 Co., Waterford, 1834, 1b.	
★ ★ ⚓	William Davis, Private, (CH), Borks, 1835	(died 7/5/68 Buried RMLI cemetery, SJI)
★ ✸ ✸ ★	John Cox, Private, 2nd. (PL), 104 Co., Devon, 1836,1b.	
★ ★	John Pearce, Private, (PO), Plymouth, Devon	
★ ★	Phillip Allen, Private, 2nd. (PL), 11 Co.,Wells, Somerset, 1834, 1b.	
★ ★	William Joy, Sergeant, 2nd. (PO), 94 Co., Dorset,1826, 1b.	
★ ★	Stephen Canning, Private, 2nd. (PO), 26 Co., Hampshire, 1827	
★ ★	Thomas Adams, Private, 2nd. (PO), 50 Co., Stafford,1836, 1b.	
★ ★	Thomas Waddington, Private, 2nd. (PO), 94 Co., Leeds, 1827, 1b.	
★ ★	William Smith, Private, 2nd (PO), 54 Co., Leicester, 1836, 1b.	
★ ✸ ★	Nehemiah Miles, Private, 2nd. (PO), 82 Co., Salisbury, Wiltshire, 1827, 1b.	
★ ★	Jabez Hancock, Private, 2nd. (PO), 18 Co., Stafford, 1837	
★ ★	William Cottrell, Private, 2nd. (PO), 101 Co., Walderton, Berkshire, 1837	

★ ★	John Prettyjohn, Colour Sergeant, 2nd. (PL), 3 Co., Devon, 1833, 3b. (Victoria Cross/Crimea)
★ ★	John Newbury, Corporal, 1st. (WO), 40 Co., Bach, 1837
★	George Hughes, Bugler, 1st. (PL), 35 Co., Devon, 1837 (Deserted 22 Dec 1861)
★ ★	John Charlton, Private, 2nd. (PL), 7 Co., Charlton, Somerset, 1822, 2b.
★ ★	George Doidge, Private, 2nd. (PL), 83 Co., Devon, 1823, 3b.
★ ★	John Hipwell, Private, 2nd. (PL), 27 Co., Leicester, 1837
★ ★	Henry Lewis, Private, 2nd. (PL), 31 Co., Somerset, 1825, 2b.
	Michael Wheland, Private, 1st. (PL), 31 Co., Kilkenny, 1826, 2b.
★ ★	Samuel Clapp, Private, 2nd. (PL), 35 Co., Somerset, 1831, 1b.
★ ★	Henry Martin, Private, 2nd. (PL), 35 Co., Somerset, 1828, 2b.
★ ★	Daniel Fussell, Private, 2nd. (PL), 59 Co., Gloucester, 1827, 2b.
★ ★	George Alderman, Private, 2nd. (PL), 63 Co., Devon, 1820, 2b.
★ ★	Henry Phipps, Private, 2nd. (PL), Hereford, 1825, 1b.
★ ★	Joseph Ellis, Private, 2nd. (PL), 91 Co., Devon, 1834, 1b. (Drowned 4/1/63, buried RM cemetery, SAJH)
★ ★	William Dymond, Private, 2nd. (PL), 75 Co., Devon, 1835, 1b.
★ ★	Francis Thyer, Private, 2nd. (PL), 79 Co., Somerset, 1831, 1b.
★ ★	George Evans, Private, 2nd. (PL), 40 Co., Devon, 1831, 1b.
★ ★	Charles Whitlock, Corporal, 1st. (PO), 26 Co., 1832, 2b.
★ ★	William Gore, Private, 2nd. (PL), 59 Co., Somerset, 1831, 1b.
★ ★	William Crowcomb, Private, 2nd. (PL), 31 Co., Devon, 1835, 1b.
★ ★	Patrick Kelly, Private, 2nd. (PL), 23 Co., Lancashire, 1834
★ ★	James Walters, Private, 2nd. (PO), 74 Co., 1829, 1b.
★ ✳ ★	William Birtwhistle, Private, 2nd. (PO), 22 Co., York, 1833
★ ★	George Kellow, Private, 2nd. (PO), 98 Co., Wiltshire, 1837
★ ✳ ★	Richard Griffin, Private, 2nd. (PL), 23 Co., Somerset, 1836, 1b.
★ ★	John Turney, Corporal, 2nd. (PO), 6 Co., London, 1833, 1b.
★ ★	John Ruttle, Private/Corporal, 2nd. (PL), 71 Co., Limerick, 1835
★	James Bowen, Private, 2nd. (PO), 71 Co., Devon, 1831, 1b.
★ ★	William Trimlin, Private, 2nd. (PO), 86 Co., Wiltshire, 1835, 1b.
★ ★	Thomas Kiddy, Private, 2nd. (CH), 21 Co., Suffolk, 1836, 1b. (Drowned 4/1/63, buried RM cemetery SAJH)

★ ✹ ★	John Taylor, Private, 2nd. (CH), 77 Co., Oxford, 1837, 1b. (1b. lost in 1859)	
★ ✹ ★	William Jeffries, Private, 1st. (CH), 49 Co., Berkshire, 1838, 1 b.	
★ ✹ ★ ★	James Haynes, Private, 1st. (CH), 41 Co., Essex, 1837, 1b.	
★ ★ ⚓	Thomas Heard, Private, (CH), 21 Co., Essex, 1830, 1 b.	
★ ★	John Edgecumbe, Private, 2nd. (PL), 99 Co., Devon, 1836	
	John Griffiths, Private, 2nd. (PL), 3 Co., Cheshire, 1831	27 May 60 San Juan Island
★ ✹ ★	Joseph Claydon, Private, 2nd. (PO), 34 Co., Oxford, 1835	27 Dec 60 Bacchante Sv. at San Juan Island
★ ★	James Hockaday, Private, 1st. (PL), 31 Co., Devon, 1834, 1 b.	
★ ★	George Webber, Private, 1st. (PL), 71 Co., Somerset, 1837 1 b.	
★ ★	George Brown, Private, 2nd. (PO), 90 Co., Leicester, 1828, 3 b.	
★ ★	John Woolley, Private, 2nd. (PL), 83 Co., Manchester, 1836	
★ ★	William Bate, Private, 1st. (PL), 95 Co., Cornwall, 1836	

New on Victualling List, Bacchante RMLI (Jan-March 1861)

	George Hobbs, Private
	Joseph Cimlis, Private
	John Payne, Private
★ ✹ ✹	George Hall, Private (On the Victualling List, HMS *Scout*, *San Juan*, October-December 1872) 38/7120
★	William Parsons, Private
★	George Gibbett, Private

New on Victualling List, HMS Bacchante, 1 Oct.—31 Dec. 1861 (38/5648)

Joseph Curtis

Victualling List, HMS Scout, 1 Oct.—31 Dec. 1872

Detachment San Juan carried on books: 88 enlisted, 3 officers, 1 assistant surgeon

WALTER JOY DIARY

Colour Sergeant Walter Joy's journal of the years 1856-1866 is archived in the Portsmouth City Museum, along with six oil paintings he did of the British Columbia coast. Sergeant Joy sailed in August 1857 on the steam Transport *Imperatrice* via Cape of Good Hope and Singapore to join the Royal Marine Light Infantry brigade then fighting at Canton. He was part of the 2nd Marine Battalion under Captain Bazalgette. He then crossed to Vancouver in HMS *Tribune*, arriving in February, 1859. Joy, along with a small detachment of 25 RMLI, under Lieutenant T.M.Cooper, were stationed at Victoria as the "Palace Guard" through July of 1859, when he was shipped to San Juan Island for the Pig War crisis. The journal is as follows:

28 July 1859 - Embarked in HMS *Tribune* and went to San Juan Island, in consequence of the Americans having landed some troops there.

19 Aug. 1859 - returned to Esquimalt after Blockade Duty at San Juan on *Tribune*.

21 March 1860 - left the barrack, Victoria, and embarked in HMS *Satellite* proceeded to San Juan Island, anchored for the night in Griffin Bay.

22 March 1860 - Weighed, and proceeded to the north end of the Island, and anchored in Rocks Bay.

23 March 1860 - Landed in a bay completely land-locked, our Camping Ground being on a shell bank - the accumulation of Years, evidently, as it averaged ten feet high, from thirty-five to forty feet through, by 120 yards long. It was the work of Indians, as they live very much on a shell-fish called "Clams", and of course deposit the shells just outside their huts, hence the bank I mentioned. The brush wood grew quite down to the water's edge, in the rear the forest was growing in undisturbed tranquility, yellow Pine, White Pine, cedar, Alder and Willows in the low flat ground are the general features of the North end of the Island.

24 March 1860 - Ceased to be Acting Sergeant Major. Made Acting Provost Sergeant.

19 May 1860 - Went away to Mr. Griffin's HBC. Got in a tide rip and nearly swamped. Obliged to put back and run the boat into a little cove and remained there all day. At sunset went outside the tide rip, swell still very heavy. After rowing about 1 1/2 miles put into a bay - beached the boat and lay there all night with Pearce and Curtis.

20 May 1860 - Myself and Pearce walked in to the HBC Station and brought out what we wanted. Made sail on the boat for camp about 2 pm. Arrived in Camp at 4:30 pm.

20 July 1861 - Went in Gun Boat Forward to Esquimalt

(At this—Joy joins the marine contingent aboard the HMS Forward until January 1862.)

15 Jan. 1862 - I returned to the Detachment on San Juan Island where I remained until 20 March, 1863.

(Joy was transferred to the HMS Devastation.)

6 Sept. 1864 - At 6:30 am proceeded to and called at San Juan Island, boats taking in stores to the camp. I called on Officers and old comrades, bidding them good-bye.

3 Oct. 1865 - At 10:45 a.m. after dropping our anchor and getting it up again, we made a final start for San Juan Island. Arrived there and anchored in Roche's Harbour at 5:45 p.m. fired a gun from a boat from Marine camp to come off, which did in about an hour with Captain Bazalgette, Governor and Captain went onshore to Marine Camp, also the master and Doctor Bogg, with myself, in cutter pulled with Marines. I found everything looking about the same as when I left it in 1863, we stopped there but a short time, as we had to be on board again before Captain. He came shortly after us when we got under weigh for Esquimalt about 3:20 p.m.

ACKNOWLEDGMENTS

———•◆•———

The author wishes to thank San Juan Island National Historical Park Superintendent Peter Dederich, Dr. Wayne Suttles, Dr. Julie Stein, Dr. Barbara Wollman, Barbara Marrett, Boyd Pratt, Candace Wellman, Gordon Smith, and Simon Sherwood for review and comment of the manuscript. Many thanks as well as to the Royal Engineers living history group of British Columbia - especially John Lansdowne, Simon Sherwood, Mark Hanus, Daryl Hall, David Funk, and Tim Watkins - for assembling a vast quantity of information about military and naval matters in the early years of the province; Rob Whitlam of the Washington State Historic Preservation Office; Roger Nixon, a commissioned researcher in London, England; Jim Adams, Mark Mackay, Ben Nechanicky, and Suzanne Greninger of NWIA; and Park Ranger Ron Garner, and all the staff and volunteers at San Juan Island NHP.

PHOTOGRAPHS and ILLUSTRATIONS

———•◆•———

Photographs and illustrations appearing on pages 1, 2, 3, 4, 14, 16, 22, 35 & 69 provided courtesy of the Yale Collection of Western Americana, Beinecke Rare Book and Manuscript Library

Appearing on pages 11, 47, 57, 71 & 77 courtesy of the Provincial Archives of British Columbia

Appearing on pages 6, 9, 13, 14, 15, 19, 20, 21, 23, 25, 27, 31, 32, 37, 41, 45, 46, 59, 60, 63, 65, 67, 73, 74, 79, 83 & 84 courtesy of the San Juan Island National Historical Park Archive, National Park Service

Appearing on page vii *Map of the Oregon Territory, 1841* id. WSU 530, courtesy of Manuscripts, Archives, and Special Collections, Washington State University Libraries, Pullman WA

INDEX

105

About the Author:

Mike Vouri is Chief Interpreter and Historian at San Juan Island National Historical Park. He is also the author of *The Pig War: Standoff at Griffin Bay*.